Praise for *The New and Collected Poems of Jane Gentry*

"Like Elizabeth Bishop, Jane Gentry is a poet of houses and family history; like Muriel Rukeyser, she is a poet of the body and the body politic. At once earthy and learned, wild and restrained, she is a poet of the whole self. Her work draws strength and subject from its Kentucky roots: Her family arrived in the time of Daniel Boone. Along with their stories, she writes of Abraham Lincoln, whom she called 'perhaps the greatest native Kentucky writer.' In her address as the state's poet laureate, she tells us, 'Stories generate soul.' Never sentimental, Gentry writes of the body as house, as garden, as dirt. In that garden, 'Our hunger itself is the fruit.' She sings of birth and grief, aging and exultation. Her figure for the artist is a white pig. 'What other / brutes,' she asks, 'could translate this / bright dirt?'"—George Ella Lyon, Poet Laureate of Kentucky (2015–2016) and author of *Many-Storied House: Poems*

"In poem after poem in this rich and important collection, Jane Gentry commemorates her personal history through the lens of poetry—family, friends, the seasons, the flora and fauna she moves through. This book is a love song to Kentucky."—Jeff Worley, author of *What Comes Down to Us: 25 Contemporary Kentucky Poets*

"Reading through her collected poems, I am again reminded that Jane Gentry was not only a master poet—but also a master teacher. The poems here, each sophisticated, precise, carefully composed, teach us how to be in the world, no matter if walking among Kentucky flowers or the fountains of Jardin du Luxembourg. In this collection, Jane continues to hold the lantern, leading us to the dark well of the past, urging us to look down so that we may see our authentic lives shimmering on the water's surface."—Kathleen Driskell, author of *Next Door to the Dead: Poems*

"Jane Gentry was a poet of uncommon grace and intelligence. To sit with these collected poems is to spend a lifetime in her gentle company. From the garden of her heart she brings us the most exquisite blooms—flowers for the living. I read and reread these poems with gratitude and deep pleasure."—Frederick Smock, author of *The Bounteous World*

THE NEW AND COLLECTED POEMS
OF JANE GENTRY

A
THOMAS
D. CLARK
MEDALLION
BOOK

The Thomas D. Clark Medallion was established to honor the memory and contributions of Dr. Thomas Dionysius Clark (1903–2005). A beloved teacher, prolific author, resolute activist, and enthusiastic advocate of publications about Kentucky and the region, Dr. Clark helped establish the University of Kentucky Press in 1943, which was reorganized in 1969 as the University Press of Kentucky, the state-mandated scholarly publisher for the Commonwealth. The Clark Medallion is awarded annually to one University Press of Kentucky publication that achieves Dr. Clark's high standards of excellence and addresses his wide breadth of interests about the state. Winners of the Thomas D. Clark Medallion are selected by the Board of Directors of the Thomas D. Clark Foundation Inc., a private nonprofit organization established in 1994 to provide financial support for the publication of vital books about Kentucky and the region.

THE NEW AND COLLECTED POEMS OF JANE GENTRY

Edited by Julia Johnson

Foreword by
Mary Ann Taylor-Hall

K UNIVERSITY PRESS OF KENTUCKY

A Garden in Kentucky (1995) and *Portrait of the Artist as a White Pig* (2006), by Jane Gentry, are reprinted here by permission of Louisiana State University Press, lsupress.org. All rights reserved.

"Night Beasts in the Backyard" was previously published in the *Louisville Review* (Fall 2013). "In October" and "March Wind" were previously published in the chapbook *A Year in Kentucky: A Garland of Poems* (Press Eight Seventeen, 2005).

Scholarly publisher for the Commonwealth,
serving Bellarmine University, Berea College, Centre
College of Kentucky, Eastern Kentucky University,
The Filson Historical Society, Georgetown College,
Kentucky Historical Society, Kentucky State University,
Morehead State University, Murray State University,
Northern Kentucky University, Transylvania University,
University of Kentucky, University of Louisville,
and Western Kentucky University.
All rights reserved.

Editorial and Sales Offices: The University Press of Kentucky
663 South Limestone Street, Lexington, Kentucky 40508-4008
www.kentuckypress.com

Cataloging-in-Publication data available from the Library of Congress

ISBN 978-0-8131-7407-5 (hardcover : alk. paper)
ISBN 978-0-8131-7408-2 (pdf)
ISBN 978-0-8131-7409-9 (epub)

This book is printed on acid-free paper meeting
the requirements of the American National Standard
for Permanence in Paper for Printed Library Materials.

∞

Manufactured in the United States of America.

Member of the Association of
American University Presses

In common things that round us lie
Some random truths he can impart,—
The harvest of a quiet eye
That broods and sleeps on his own heart.

—William Wordsworth, from "A Poet's Epitaph"

Contents

Portrait of the Artist as a White Pig

I

III

Late Poems

I

II

III

Foreword

This is a brilliant book, the life's work of one who was profoundly aware of the oddness and richness of her life. I believe it will be read far into the future, not only here in Kentucky, where it is so passionately rooted, but wherever people honor the exploration of what it means to be fully alive, fully human. The poems are musing and reflective, but they also can be (often simultaneously) bawdy and rambunctious and sensual—joyful, angry, lustful, grief stricken.

What's in these pages is an act of radical generosity, an uncensored record of a life lived and treasured by someone with an ardent, receptive spirit, someone capable of penetrating—that is, finding words that led her toward the full apprehension of—her experience, its truth. She lived deeply, felt at home in her own world, and went out into the larger one not as a visitor to it but as a citizen of it. She was, to quote Henry James, *one on whom nothing is lost.*

For about twenty-five years, Jane and six other women—Donna Boyd, Carolyn Hisel, Susan Richards, Audrey Robinson, Judy Young, and myself—met every third week, bringing with us whatever we'd made in the interim, in the forms we used—poetry, fiction, painting, sculpture, music—in response to three words we had drawn out of a box at the previous meeting. It was a game, a way to get back to the first, innocent intentions of our artistic lives, when we were children—to do what we liked, to be free, to express what we were feeling, without worrying about whether it was any good, whether we were embarrassing ourselves. A way to have fun, not to care too much about judgment, success, ambition. Just to play. We called this gathering, when we called it anything, *art group*. No capital letters. We had a good time together, and as it happened, in spite of (or maybe because of) our modest intentions, some amazing work transpired. Many of Jane's poems from *art group* are included in this collection. Jane couldn't be there for every meeting—unlike the rest of us, she had a demanding job and, in the early years, two girls at home—but when she was with us, the discourse became maybe a little more serious. Her eye was keen and her responses trustworthy, coming from a spirit both refined and completely, unabashedly up for anything.

The poems here presented are the work of a poet who has occupied and tended her life as if it were an exasperating, delightful, eccentric, beloved house that has been in the family for generations. They are the work of a discerning woman who knew how to treasure what was before her that deserved to be treasured.

Mary Ann Taylor-Hall

Introduction

The poems of Jane Gentry are bold, original, and precise. Their voice is that of a poet deeply rooted in place. Whether the setting is a wide landscape or the small space of a room, we share in Jane Gentry's unexpected observations and follow the rhythm of her speaking voice. Each poem reveals something new, always with clarity and astonishingly lyrical grace.

Jane Gentry was born in Lexington, Kentucky, on February 9, 1941, and raised on a farm in Athens, Kentucky. Her parents were Charles Blanding Gentry and Dixie Walker Gentry. Her forebears had lived in the area of Athens since the time of the settlement at Boonesborough—the very time period that Daniel Boone was there. Her maternal grandfather, Clarence Walker, was pastor of Ashland Avenue Baptist Church in Lexington from 1916 through 1966.

Gentry received her bachelor's degree in English literature from Hollins College (Phi Beta Kappa); her master's in English from Brandeis University in Massachusetts, where she was a Woodrow Wilson Fellow; and her PhD from the University of North Carolina at Chapel Hill. She returned to Kentucky to join the faculty of the University of Kentucky Honors Program and to establish the program's literary magazine. A forty-year resident of Versailles, Kentucky, she was a beloved English professor, teaching poetry workshops in the Department of English and courses on the history of ideas in the university's Honors Program, until her retirement in 2013. Of the influence of teaching on her as poet, she said, "In my work as a teacher in the Honors Program at the University of Kentucky, I have taught the Greeks and Romans in translation for so long that the myths and other kinds of stories out of those cultures come into my poems just as my memories from childhood do."

Gentry recalled her childhood to colleague, longtime friend, and fellow former poet laureate of Kentucky Gurney Norman in an interview: "When I was a child it was usual to see a team of mules in a field plowing or pulling a mower or a rake. Everybody had a milk cow. Everybody had chickens that they gathered eggs from. By the time I was twenty you didn't see that anymore, but I feel really lucky to have gotten a feel for what that was like in that time before that turning." Of the poems in her 2006 collection, *Portrait of the Artist as a White Pig,* she said, "I think [the poems] see the natural world as the context of our lives even though modern conditions remove us, place us at a remove from the natural world. Some of the poems, particularly ones about family, recognize the sacredness of human character, celebrating, for example, how a woman who has found a way to be her truest self can be a linchpin in her world."

In a WRFL public radio interview with poet Katerina Stoykova-Klemer, Gentry said of her process: "The making of a poem begins for me when I am struck by some resonance between my own inner being and the outer world." Of *Portrait of the Artist as a White Pig,* she said, "These poems are about everyday events and feelings in an ordinary life. I think I tend to focus on moments of insight, even—sometimes, I hope, revelation—when human experience sheds its protective mask of ordinariness and exposes the bright bones of time itself, of the sureness of death, and the quick beauty that such conditions make possible."

Gentry chose Hollins College because her father said she could go "anywhere she wanted to as long as it was a girls' school in Virginia," but also because she knew she could take a creative writing workshop as a freshman. And so, beginning in 1959 with a poetry workshop, she studied English and creative writing at Hollins, publishing her first poems in 1963 while still a student. According to R. H. W. Dillard, longtime director of the Hollins Creative Writing Program, Gentry held her own among graduate students in the program as one of the advanced undergraduates. The workshop, taught by Louis D. Rubin Jr., founder of the Hollins Creative Writing Program, was held weekly in the evening at Rubin's home on the campus's faculty row. Both Nobel laureate William Golding and Howard Nemerov, winner of a National Book Award and a Pulitzer Prize, sat in on the workshop while serving as writers-in-residence at Hollins; Golding in 1962 and Nemerov in 1963.

In 1968, Louis Rubin accepted a position at the University of North Carolina at Chapel Hill. He and Gentry met again at Chapel Hill during Gentry's Ph.D. studies, after she had completed a master's degree at Brandeis and spent a year working as a reporter for the *Lexington Leader*. Louis Rubin continued to be an invaluable friend and mentor, and the two exchanged letters on the subjects of poetry and family for many years. Of Rubin, Gentry once noted, "The single most important teacher who helped me think of myself as a poet is critic and novelist Louis D. Rubin Jr., who was my mentor when I was an undergraduate at Hollins and when I was a graduate student at the University of North Carolina. He had the gift of being able to see clearly what a writer is trying to do and to tell her what she needs to do to make the work better."

In the early 1990s I was an undergraduate English major with a concentration in creative writing at Hollins College. It was during those years that I first heard the name Jane Gentry Vance (her married name, used by friends and colleagues). Gentry was one of the legendary Hollins poets of the 1960s and one of the distinguished Hollins writers I hoped one day to meet, whose ranks included Sylvia Wilkinson, Elizabeth Seydel Morgan, Lee Smith, Elizabeth Forsythe Hailey, Henry Taylor, and Annie Dillard—all students of Rubin. Unfortunately, I did not have the opportunity to meet Gentry during my undergraduate years, but I am grateful to have begun a friendship with her in 2011, when I joined the creative writing faculty in the Department of English at the University of Kentucky. Gentry was an accomplished, respected, and supportive senior colleague, and, as a fellow woman poet in the department, she was a loyal friend.

This collection includes two full-length collections of poetry in their entirety: *A Garden in Kentucky* (Louisiana State University Press, 1995) and *Portrait of the Artist as a White Pig* (Louisiana State University Press, 2006). *A Garden in Kentucky* spans many years and contains work published while Gentry was still a student at Hollins. *Portrait of the Artist as a White Pig,* published in 2006, includes poems written during the ten years that followed.

This collection also includes, in the section titled "Late Poems," a substantial number of Gentry's unpublished poems, for the most part written in the period from 2006 until the end of her life, in 2014. In 2005, Press 817 in Lexington, Kentucky, brought out her chapbook *A Year in Kentucky.* Two poems published in the chapbook, "In October" and "March Wind," were not included in *Portrait of the Artist as White Pig,* but they can be found in the "Late Poems" section of this collection.

Gentry left behind many unpublished poems; it is not clear if she intended the poems to be published as a single manuscript. Since many of the poems are undated, I have arranged "Late Poems" into four sections on the basis of thematic principles. Additionally, I have a selected a few early unpublished poems for inclusion. When possible, I tried to use Gentry's own methodology for arranging poems within the sections, following sequences analogous to those found in her previous collections. Although Gentry's writing displays stylistic changes over the course of her career, its hallmark remains constant: insight into nature, faith, the quotidian, and—perhaps most prominently—the grounding of her home and family in the state of Kentucky. These themes do not exist in isolation; they overlap in complex ways throughout the work.

Section three of "Late Poems" is perhaps the clearest in its thematic organization, following clues in Gentry's original manuscripts. These poems, many of which Gentry saved as files called "Bill poems," address directly and chronicle the illness of William H. Strode III, her beloved companion of ten years and a Pulitzer Prize–winning photographer, who died of cancer in 2006. In some instances, there are two versions of a poem. In these cases, I selected a version based on the kinds of revision decisions Gentry seems to have made in her published poems, of which she often saved two or more alternate drafts. My hope is that the final arrangement serves to showcase the range of Gentry's work and the flexibility of her style: sometimes incorporating a sense of ironic humor, sometimes poignant; and always clear, intelligent, and revelatory. When asked about the collection *Portrait of the Artist as a White Pig,* Gentry said, "I write poems when I have to write poems. So the things that move me in that particular way, things of the earth and of my experience, come to me in a shape that wants to be made into a poem—they have a kinship naturally and so I think from the very beginning of the making of these poems, I had a sense that they were moving towards a shape that was going to be a book." The poems collected herein share kinship expressed not just in their shapes but also in their voice, a voice irrevocably her own.

During her lifetime, Gentry's poems appeared widely in journals, including the *Sewanee Review,* the *Hollins Critic, Harvard Magazine, New Virginia Review, Southern Poetry Review,* the *Greensboro Review,* and the *American Voice,* and were published in numerous anthologies, including *Hero's Way: Contemporary Poems in the Mythic Tradition* (Prentice-Hall), *Cries of the Spirit: A Celebration of Women's Spirituality* (Beacon Press), *Elvis in Oz* (University Press of Virginia), *The American Voice Anthology of Poetry* (University Press of Kentucky), *The Yellow Shoe Poets: 1964–1999* (Louisiana State University Press), and *What Comes Down to Us: 25 Contemporary Kentucky Poets* (University Press of Kentucky).

As a critic, Gentry published articles on the work of Louis D. Rubin, Mary Oliver, Mary Lee Settle, Sylvia Wilkinson, and Madison Cawein, among others, along with dozens of reviews, essays, and interviews appearing in such journals and anthologies as *Southern Literary Quarterly, Mississippi Quarterly, Iron Mountain Review, American Women Writing Fiction: Memory, Identity, Family, Space, Encyclopedia of American Poetry: The Nineteenth Century* and *Encyclopedia of American Poetry: The Twentieth Century.* Her dissertation was on the work of Howard Nemerov. Additionally, she wrote, with William M. Lamb, a volume of local history, *Looking Back at Athens* (1985), and in 2008 coedited the anthology *Five Kentucky Poets Laureate,* designed to introduce high school students to contemporary Kentucky poetry.

Gentry received numerous awards for her work, including two Al Smith Fellowships from the Kentucky Arts Council and residency fellowships from Yaddo in Saratoga Springs, New York, and the Virginia Center for Creative Arts in Lynchburg. She was the winner of the University of Kentucky Alumni Association's Great Teacher Award, an honor she especially prized since it was nominated and awarded by students. Gentry served as Kentucky Poet Laureate in 2007–2008, traveling the state advocating for the importance of literature as part of the culture and history of Kentucky. In 2008, when she organized and introduced a reading at the Library of Congress in Washington, DC, she featured three

Kentucky poets—Tony Crunk, Maurice Manning, and Davis Mc-Combs—whose first books were individually selected for the Yale Series of Younger Poets competition. In 2009 she read a poem ("Alexander Gardner's November 8, 1963 Photograph of Lincoln") at the Kennedy Center in Washington, DC, honoring the bicentennial of President Lincoln's birth as part of the Kentucky Humanities Council's "Our Lincoln." In May 2013, Gentry was awarded Hollins University's Distinguished Alumnae Award. In October 2013, she was inducted into the UK College of Arts and Sciences Hall of Fame, the highest honor awarded by the college. She served as a member of the vestry at St. John's Episcopal Church in Versailles. Jane Gentry Vance died of cancer on October 2, 2014.

Gentry's daughters, Lucy Vance Seligson, an accomplished Broadway singer and now a clinical social worker for the Actors Fund, and Susannah Vance Gopalan, an attorney specializing in health care law and policy, are central to this collection. Her daughters and grandchildren are constant figures in poems such as "Susannah," "Susannah's Bones," "Leaving Lucy, September, 1990," "Sitting with Aunt Mary in Hospice," "My Two Daughters in Paris," and "My Grown Daughters Asleep in the Same Bed." Susannah and Lucy gathered the unpublished poems together in manuscript form and from the hard drive of Gentry's computer. I am exercising my editorial liberty to dedicate this collection to her three grandchildren, Jacob Walker Seligson, Andrew Vance Seligson, and Uma Jane Gopalan. Uma was born in October 2014, three weeks after Gentry's death.

Gentry's poems are startling, marvelous, and heart-wrenching. Many of her later poems seem to be in direct conversation with death as she moved closer to it. But the elegiac lyrics on the death of a lover, or of a friend, or on Gentry's own approaching death, bravely faced, reveal a poet who was always deeply optimistic and full of faith and love. Gentry's final poems, on family and on place, ask the reader to examine the contexts that shape them. In "A Nap in Summer," we are brought into a room with familiar faces from Gentry's world, including a picture of her grandson Jake on his first birthday, a photograph of Bill, and fading sunlight touching the land she knew and loved so well: "a path of light that drops beyond the ridge." Our sight is refreshed by Jane Gentry's keen eye—one whose perceptions are striking and true, brimming with stunning, unexpected beauty.

Julia Johnson

A Garden in Kentucky
(1995)

Mrs. Copperfield put her hand
over her heart. "Le bonheur," she
whispered, "le bonheur . . . what an
angel a happy moment is—"

—Jane Bowles, *Two Serious Ladies*

I

What are they looking at? Is it the river?
The sunlight on the river, the summer, leisure,
Or the luxury and nothingness of consciousness?

—Delmore Schwartz, "Seurat's 'Sunday
Afternoon Along the Seine' "

A Garden in Kentucky

Under the fluorescent sun
inside the Kroger, it is always
southern California. Hard avocados
rot as they ripen from the center out.
Tomatoes granulate inside their hides.
But by the parking lot, a six-tree orchard
frames a cottage where winter has set in.

Pork fat seasons these rooms.
The wood range spits and hisses,
limbers the oilcloth on the table
where an old man and an old woman
draw the quarter-moons of their nails,
shadowed still with dirt,
across the legends of seed catalogues.

Each morning he milks the only goat
inside the limits of Versailles. She feeds
a rooster that wakes up all the neighbors.
Through dark afternoons and into night
they study the roses' velvet mouths
and the apples' bright skins
that crack at the first bite.

When thaw comes, the man turns up
the sod and, on its underside, ciphers
roots and worms. The sun like an angel
beats its wings above their grubbing.

Evenings on the viny porch they rock,
discussing clouds, the chance of rain.
Husks in the dark dirt fatten and burst.

The Drum Majorette Marries
at Calvary Baptist

She goes blind down the aisle.
Candles prick the twilight
banks of gladioli, fern, and baby's breath.
Abloom in polyester peau de soie,
she smiles a starlet smile, clings
to her wet-eyed daddy's beef.
The organ metes her steps in groans.
Her mother wrings a tissue in her lap.
The groom, monolith to the white cloud
she is, waits at the altar. His Adam's
apple bobs. He is a straight, black
prop incidental to this script.

Outside, night falls over the tableau
the flashbulbs freeze as the couple
ducks through showers of seed
and runs for the idling limousine.
Before the door clicks shut on all her gauze,
in the strange light the white dress
seems to drift like petals piece by piece,
until out of the net the drum majorette
pumps her knees. Her trim boots dart,
her white gloves slice
at cacophonies of dark.
Her silver whistle flashes, shrills.

Grandfather Lights the Gas Stove

Grandfather breathed fire from the pulpit
and flames sat on their heads in cloven tongues.
At home, he brought white-eyed potatoes
from the pantry dark with its secret smells
of old walnuts and Bible leather.
Wearing Maugie's apron, he washed pans
and spoke earnestly to his own face
in the looking glass over the sink.

Into the bright hell of the barrel-bellied
stove, he fed the chunks of coal.
The air, sweet with heat, awash
with the clock's regular voice,
settled over us in a blessing.
Stretched on the daybed, he meditated
on the Acts of the Apostles,
the intoxicant of Pentecost. The Bible,
open across his stomach, soon rose
with his breath, his building snores.

Hooded, he comes at dawn, hunkers,
opens the valve, and the breath
of gas hisses, explodes across
the white row of teeth. Slowly
the hundreds of asbestos tongues
stir to life in the new blue fire,
and his shadow rears and leaps

across the ceiling, arches over
the cold-faced girls budding
together inside the comforter.

Maugie's Heaven

In June at sunrise robins roof
my house with nesty noises: chirrup
chirrup, the bright trees
branch into my sleep.
Once, a child on Maugie's porch,
I slept while flocks, hosts
of robins, chorused mother music
that spilled my eyes onto the bed,
the floor, the new-plowed fields
like water swelling
the year to summer.

This June new robins shout,
celebrating sky, not heaven
or lost sheep, creatures
of grass, the closed kingdom,
their bodies ripening toward
the fold that Maugie knows.
Lying deep in spring
lapped in hymns of dirt
beneath the teeth of grass,
she dreams that robins sing
their lust above her empty
house, the bed she made,
among hallelujahs of new leaves.

Aunt Lucy

As pure at ninety-four as any babe
newborn, Aunt Lucy died. She loved
a maiden's pleasures: purple, funerals,
young company, blooming hats, Jesus.
At Easter church, without an orchid
to her name, she would survey
the flowering bosoms and chastely
dream a dark-dyed purple of her own.

In Lucy's bright-eyed, backward mind,
eighty years ago was near as now: jigging
through lamplight into daylight, she frisked
her mare all day, outrode her posting,
untied beaux, until she galloped her cane to bed,
vowing she wouldn't last through winter.

Now that stones are cold, trees naked,
gardens brittle, she sleeps like a baby,
clutching a queer blossom, trundled away
under the beds of tulips and the plots of daffodils,
tucked in beneath the blank of snow
where bulbs smolder between sheets of ice.

Planted with her first and only orchid,
Lucy winters through, her old-maid mind,
feeble as February sun, recollecting snow.
Let her hold out for some combustion of that bloom
whose shoots may yet fire spring

when the cold comforter melts—
her and her rootless flower.
For they lie here and, under cover of death,
sleep a short sleep.

Great-Grandfather's Dog, High, on a Tintype

On a sunny porch he lies,
head on paws, eyes strangely lighted,
forlorn among failing images:
empty rocker, child in the door,
sun squares on old planks.
A dog in a brown study,
he lies still in the tintype
losing itself to light.
On the back, words stay
as Maugie wrote them:
     "Papa's dog. High.
     He laid here until he died waiting for Papa.
     He would not eat. He loved him."

I see the dog
circle slowly after his tail
on the warm boards and settle
for this posture of loyalty,
bleaching now white as bones
buried in the yard.
High hoards all his bones,
bones lost to earth
bones of his master
his master's child
after the lightened breath
mumbles them all clean
after the sun's tongue
licked this picture.

The Old Place
1949

Sun pools
under the high trees
in the leafy rooms
birds crisscross
their songs.
Up the cliff, crows
fire war cries
at each other.
Men and women slap
cards on the table,
laugh, holler.
The creek
cold, mud-sucking
fresh and mossy
arcs with crawdads,
minnows. Boys
and girls skate
its slick floor
balancing like
tightrope walkers,
arms outstretched.
Pepsi-Colas frosted
in the ice chest.
Warm sweet beans,
Mary's potato salad.
Chicken fried
to crumbled bites.

Across the valley
the red-and-white barn
breathes cool
silky tobacco dust.
Around the white-
washed outhouse
mud daubers write
in terrifying loops
the script of this day
so bright, invisible.

Washing Sheets in July

Thin clouds work the sheet of sky—
jays cry, flat and starchy.
Against the white garage
hollyhocks flicker.
The sheets, wet, adhesive
as I hang them, smell
of soap and bee-filled air.

Flags of order in the palpable sun,
how they snap in the new breeze!
Watching them balloon on the line,
I swell with an old satisfaction:
I beat them clean in the Euphrates.
Poems half-conceived drift off—
unwritten essays muddle, fade.
The white sheets crack in the wind,
fat bellies of sails,
sweet as round stomachs of children.

Tonight they'll carry me to sleep
in joy, in peace,
muscles unknotting, tired eyes clearing
in the dark under their lids.
The sheets, fragrant as summer,
carry me into realms of cleanliness,
deep dreams of order.

Teddy

September sun checkers his yard.
His bearded, crowned chickens
peck and sing in the fencerow.
His angles of bone collapse
into the green yard chair;
its metal back splays like a tulip.
This moment of comfort blooms
on his slack yellow skin.

"Uncle Teddy," I say, "Daddy
has to have the operation. It is
cancer." His breath curls,
the day darkens
through the membrane of tears.
I clasp the back of his hand
on the rusty chair arm;
his five hard hand bones
separate in my palm.

For My Father

Athens, Kentucky

Bridge
When you rode in from your fields
I climbed your back
that spanned the forests of clover.
An airplane droned over us, so new
to the sky that we stopped falling and rolling
to look, shading our eyes.
There was no time then,
only that noon of blossoms, bees.

River
On the ride to the hospital
you were ruddy, joking,
pungent as your hatband.

Your roommate's leg,
numbed for a vasectomy,
fell off the bed.
You rolled out laughing
to pick it up.

A nurse ordered you down.
Wired to a gauge, your heart
became viscera.

After they brought you back
split like a melon,

I slipped into the doorframe
and saw Mother, eyes shut, in a chair
beside your head, holding
to the post of your bed,
a boat on a river
frothing, tumbling,
carrying you off.

Back
On the back porch
your coveralls slump
from their nail.
By the shed
your pickup
settles into the grass.
I rub your back.
Off the rack of your ribs
my fingers lift your skin,
an old shirt.

Hand
After the long failure of his farmer's body,
after the undertakers wrestled him,
zipped in plastic like last season's clothes,
past the kitchen table, out the back door,
and fed him into the black mouth of the hearse,
after the last warmth of his head
went out like an ember on his pillow, I left.

As a train carried me into London

I saw him look up from some hammering beside the track,
his shapeless cap pushed back.
He waved an old-gloved hand at me
familiar as sunlight
and opened his joyful smile
in a greeting I was already past.

Breath
I move away in time from where he left me.
When I am tired now, my face hangs from my cheekbones;
my eyes when I catch them are sad.
This old woman hid in my bones until he died,
whose arm lifted me up
to smell the sweet breath of his horse.

After Rain
He wore weather like an old sweater,
next to his skin. He watched the sky
as one searches the face of a friend.
He heard voices in the rain on the roof.
The wind spoke to him in his own breath.
He heard the language corn speaks
growing under the July sun.
He knew the appetites of dirt,
how it eats the burst seeds.

Tonight wind thrashes the bones of trees,
and rain from the west veins my window.
All his breaths are in this wind.
The earth of his grave drinks the rain

that beats on his heart and makes it grow.
Tomorrow, within fencerows he knew
by heart (the double wild cherry,
the elm stump, the rock fence corner),
his cattle, sleek in their tight skins,
will make the grass shriek with their green teeth.

Thinking of Charlie B. on July 4

In the city of the dead
Charlie B. is yet
a model citizen,
he who loved his life,
who loved, like a cat,
a patch of sunlight
to lie in, who wished
to be no one but himself,
to be nowhere
but where he was,
doing what he was doing.

Surely such a man
on the Fourth of July
enjoys his state,
his grave open
to all earth's weathers,
his atoms dancing
out into the summer night
to the rhythm of cicadas
singing, "Body, Body, Body,"
so black to the touch, ecstatic,
always weaving a new skin
for that old drum of darkness,
"Body, Body, Body," which marches
us all into that new city.

Snow in the Cemetery

At nightfall snow showers upon me from a sky
luminous as porcelain yellow pink.
Discrete as minutes of a heavy hour,
flakes, adhesive to my coat and scarf,
weight down dark symmetries of evergreen
and feather all the reaches of the bare-branched trees.

This accumulation freezes all I know.
And yet my mother lies in her new grave
under this blanket white and sudden
as the sheets she cracked out and smoothed
and tucked over the beds of my childhood,
peaceful as these hummocks under quiet snow.

My Mother's Clothes

On a December night
I brought them
from her nursing home,
forgot them on the porch
under stars brittle with cold.
I left them hanging, far
from the warmth
of her body, away from fires
that keep the winter from us.
Her clothes, familiar to me
as her skin: the wool plaid
dress she made; her favorite
jacket, hunter green,
with its lapel pin, DWG,
my father gave her—
the shape of the body
holding as they swung
from their shoulders
on the porch, arms empty
against the weather.

Tasks

I look in the mirror and see my father's face.
A thousand times before I've looked and seen
my own. But my father does live in the wilderness
of my heart, in a hidden cottage,
where the door sometimes opens into the vines
and he steps out to assess the sky,
to look for rain. Rarely, my mother appears
on the threshold, holding a plate or an apple.
They live there forever, moving through the day's tasks,
sacred and eternal to the eyes of a child:

> lighting the lamp
> pouring the water
> stirring the pot
> opening the window
> folding the cloth
> smoothing the bed
> drawing off the shoe

Presences

I thought my father callous, my mother hard,
and my grandfather unfeeling above all
for not being wretched when an old road moved
or when a house or barn would burn or fall.

That far child loved old things,
worshiped past because she had none.
But to change from child, she learned
as those who got her learned:
when sight goes empty through the vacant air—
the landmark gone—
its absence is more ancient than its being there.

II

I have a small
daughter called
Cleis, who is

like a golden
flower

I wouldn't
take all Croesus'
kingdom with love
thrown in, for her

—Sappho

A Photograph of Hollins Abroaders Before the Caryatids

Thirty years and it will be a different picture.
Husbands do set houses on girls' heads,
hair turns as gray as rock,
and eyes in made-up faces take the stony look.
They travel but they never learn
as do those ponderous maids beneath the rock.
Worn down by the gravity of time,
but serving still, held by the common chore,
they understand the stone that keeps them down.

LIFE, June, 1944,
Featuring the Bayeux Tapestry

In a quiet courtyard, dead Germans
and the rump of a grazing horse
seen through the gap in the side of a shed.
Along a Norman beach, open graves
with two empty boots by each.
And the waves stopped by the camera.
An ad for silverware: a cottage, rose-covered,
behind a girl and her soldier holding hands,
leaning on a picket fence. They swear
they'll meet again before the sterling tarnishes.
Past all this, the feature in the back,
the record of a war sewn by a queen,
what Matilda knew of William's conquest.
Along two hundred feet of rotting linen
throngs of horses thread among each other;
amid the cotton clash of swords on shields
the warriors dump their heads along the margins
go on needling, fighting their embroidered war.

The Cricket in
the Elevator Shaft

. . . sustains only a small poem:
the chirping rises
ancient as bedrock
from the pit
we dangle over
where our lifeline
crawls into its upward pull

Down there, the cricket
saws its legs,
sings
steady as stars

A Moment in the Dark

I switched off the light and put the child in bed.
As I tucked blankets round his feet, he said
in fright, finding my face with his hand,
"For a moment in the dark, Jane Gentry,
I thought you were an old lady." And
for a moment in the dark, I shall be.

For H., Resolved into a Moth While Watching Television in the Next Room

One night I was running through the backyard
of my dream, pulling from the hungry suck
of mud and tangling grass. The wind pushed hard
against strong, flapping sheets of rain that struck
and hissed upon one window filled with light.
Firm in the house's buckling, wheezing walls
which breathed the wind, a tall door took my sight,
and entering I wound straight through hollow halls.

The room, except for one bare bulb, was blank.
To nowhere, in a corner, stairs climbed high,
and at the top a tight sac flopped and sank
until a moth burst out: that monstrous fly,
as if the shaggy brown cocoon had bled,
rose damp and ruddy to batter at my head.

Hound

I am a girl of sense
and all day, as sure as sunshine,
I know you love me.
All day I stay ahead of the hound
dragging his jowls raw
to keep his nostrils in my scent.
When he snuffles up behind
I turn quick and outfox him;
my strategy's to keep him
dizzy on the daily round.
But that old dog's not dumb.
He knows the whiff of jealousy,
stays with that stench
until he tracks me down.
When I've run against the night,
am flat against my bed,
I'm forced to serve him.
Settling happy-tailed at my bedside
he ravels at my glistening guts
until we're mumbled fleshless into sleep
where love and hate are splintery bones
among the broken towers of his teeth.

Liberty Above New Haven
The Statue on East Rock

Pointing the stone needle
stitching up the looseness
of the day, she strikes against
the abstract of a sky so definitely
empty, cold, and clean
that I could wish for such a hard
and spotless place to lean.

Ten Years Ago You Left and Now We Take a Walk Together

We step
from patch to patch
of moon,
dry rocks over a spring creek.
All the mouths of night
music together.
We hold hands
familiar as crotches
of old trees.
We look through
lighted windows laughing
at the lives.
Near the end of the block
a naked woman
plump in front
of her open door
irons a shirt:
her breasts swing
over the moving heat.
We swallow the moon
what a pill
and head home.

Scarecrow

I ran you out of my garden long ago,
thought I was rid of you for good.
But now you straggle back
like a November fly bumping the cold pane.
What I married, I love:
my house, my garden, trees, children.
Yet you, ragged bird, dirty old crow,
come back here out of season,
your horny beak
slicing at my roots.
My daughter rides my leg
and hides inside my skirt.
My husband is cast down,
picks at his supper, skulks.
The dog and cats
tuck tails between their legs
and sniff their food.
Only you, gobbler,
ransack, ravage, waste our garden.
You stick like a fly at the eye
of a cow in August
until I hang a pie tin in the tree,
an empty eye to knife sun into you,
and dress a man of sticks
in my ruffled purple blouse
you always liked,
my husband's hat and work gloves dangling.

The scarecrow stands there
and, death for his familiar,
cannot die. He serves.
You come no more.

Blizzard

Tonight snow
showers flake
by flake through
the streetlight's
funnel, settles
its particulars
in billows
that snake around
the island
of our house
in the white dark.

Quiet in bed
under rafters
that float the weight
of snow above us
we drift
from this warm orbit
wave after wave
we cross into each
other, seep
into the void
particles colliding
dancing Shiva's dance
dreaming the dream
of the eye seeing
all itself
blinded in sleep

wind hurls the light
flakes into white surfs
stretching the empty fields
around our house.

Morning comes and a wash of blue
fire carries us home
from every facet of the world
crystal splinters arrow the eye
the day's one sun we always rise to.

Moving

Going back
to sweep up
broken crayons, brown
apple cores, nail parings,
I feel the ghosts
fritter in the clear
space where the sofa was,
dissolve into the wall
where the refrigerator stood.
The whites of my eyes see
them shift about the ceiling.

With all we own
gone, puzzled
like a jigsaw in the van,
the empty rooms hold
what we can't clear out
and leave here.

Your Vacation

Your absence floods the house
like dark at night
washing through closets, drawers, boxes,
seeping between the clock and the wall,
books and their spines

and my need sings
out on it
like these cicadas
screaming
behind banks of summer's black old leaves.

Susannah

I

Beetle on its back,
hooked fish on the bank,
paddling through air
in her crib,
she reaches out.
Seeing my breasts,
her eyes light
at known geography.

I am
what
I am:
perfect answer
to her appetite.
Empty O
of her mouth
eats my nipple,
her quick tongue flickers,
a snake in its hole.

The suck
of her
deep kiss
pulls me in,
she draws me,
tide to moon.
I flow to her,

locks open
I fall
to her level
in peace.

II

I rode the pig
push
when she came,
grunt, grunt
root, root
an animal snorted
deep in the swell
of my gut,
wave after wave
till sluices
opened
and out through my circles
she poured.

A sac she'd filled,
I ricocheted
around that room,
an emptying balloon
on the loose
caroming
off the cold lights,
battering at the green-
masked faces,
riding the red jet

her body washed
from mine.

III

Susannah
is
the name
I give this vacancy
this vacuum
I rush into
like wind
scrolled into thunder
when lightning scribbles
voids
across the sky.
Bug, fish, snake, pig,
she is
primordial.
In the jelly of her flesh
there is no bone.

I am
her spine, her shell,
her wing, her teeth,
her beak, her claw.

In love she breaks me
over the back
of the dark
she came from.

Susannah's Bones

When she was newborn
the hard S of her body
cracked, the vertebrae
giving as I lifted her.

I thought I'd dropped a stitch,
had let my faults undo her—
the getting too offhand,
milk scanted, vitamins missed.

For years, then, my sleep
listened for her bones.
At 3 a.m. she'd find me
in the dark, whispering,

"Mama," filling the black room.
But as her small body tossed
beside me, while I fought dreams
of fault in the marrow,

her bone knobs bloomed,
her white joints flowered
like popped corn. Her sockets
succulent, tender kernels.

St. Lucy the Housekeeper

Today I wash my windows inside
to make the most of the year's old sun.
With my own hands I keep this house,
live quietly, darkly, day by day,
sometimes finding casements open
onto odd landscapes, pasts not mine,
the empty walls cracking
in zigzags like eggs.

December is my season,
winter's dark when I was born.
Then my house draws close its shawl
of dust, images flower the walls,
my viny rugs grow lush,
and my rich old relative, Memory,
dies, pouring into my apron
bright new-minted coin.

Zero

The temperature is five above.
From the attic window
I see rooftops dimming
in the last light. The wind sulks,
cut by old bones of trees
which yearn like grass
into the moving sky.
Snow rains.
Streetlights awaken here, now there.
A front window lamp winks on.
Night falls like black water.
Against the world's shapes
and the warm human interiors
darkness at this moment shows its face.

Things That Fly Overhead
at Lake Malone

In the dark, on my back
on the sun-warmed dock,
I am surprised by what comes
between me and the night sky's
obsolete face.
A plane's red eye winks.
Its rumble burrs a comfort
to the sharp songs of the tree frogs.
A bat boomerangs after gnats, sometimes
so close I make out horns and pointed wings.
Then, way up, a firefly fades, so deep in black
I see it first as a star, light-years away.

Leaving Lucy, September, 1990

"You'll never have to worry
about that one," Jean once said,
as Lucy, the princess
in my prom dress
and bridesmaid's tiara,
squared herself between
the timid ghost and cat
to receive her treat
at the dark door.

This afternoon I leave her
in New York. I am ready.
Her new comforter is on her bed.
Her texts are bought and stand
like a rainbow on her shelf.

At the hotel, we close our bags,
find the key, double-check her schedule.
She cries beside her father on the sofa.
Because my body hollows and my hands
begin to flame, I leave the room.
I say I'll look under the beds.

Alone, I sink into the bed.
The room blackens around me.
My eyes fall
into their own emptiness.
I am a child. Long ago

someone is leaving me alone.
It is dark. A door closes.
Cicadas shake the night trees.

Lucy meets me in the doorway,
come to see what's wrong.
The tears we cry are old.
We are not two bodies.

As I pull away from the curb
she blurs. Her shape
in the rearview mirror
moves toward its own door.

In a Chinese Landscape

From the creek the bullfrog's voice opens the night
cicadas scrape the rhythm of dog days
out of the dry trees the moon climbs
into the purple of evening.
Far away my father lies withering on his bed.

My heart is full as the moon's circle
now orange and palpable
it will rise and the dark will swallow it
shrinking to a sliver
in the shadow of earth.

Two Flowers for My Father

That spring there were floods.
The summer was dry as a fever.
In October, fall still hadn't come
when the undertaker hauled his body
out under the close stars.

Now tobacco sweetens the air
of the creek bottom. Ice curdles
the barnlot puddles.
But on the back hill, a Queen Anne's lace
frames its bloody center in a clutch of briers,
and between hedge roots on the creek bank
a snapdragon, blue and deep
as sky, opens its old throats.

On a Day of Beautiful Clouds

. . . after three days of rain, I drive east
on I-64 into a sky broken open like an egg,
pouring a shine new as the first day
into my eyes. The trees, fat with summer
rain, bulge over the road, then open
to a tent of sky as blue as sea, where
just above the landline, separate clouds
swim like fish into ultramarine.
Straight up, the scrubbed-out sky
is clean as the yellow-washed world
that rolls beneath my tires.
I pass a man, white-headed, grand as God,
standing in a yard as rapt, relieved,
absorbed as if in pissing, his face lighted,
wiped clear by this depth of sky, this beaming.

III

. . . what every child knows: that nothing is ever
suffered in plural.

There is only one body. Only one death.

—Stephen Mitchell, "Pascal's Vision"

Telemakhos at Festival Market Thinks of His Father

How strange that your bones, four blocks away
under these rosy, peaceful clouds,
carried upon themselves the familiar
house of my childhood, your body.
Your oar may as well have been a winnowing fan
for all the good it finally did you.
Only the lost know your words as truth:
though you find a house of gold,
it cannot be as sweet as your own house
or the house of your parents.
Now as I eat my supper in this mall
I listen to the murmur of artificial
falls and to the tunes Calliope plays
as she turns some children on the carrousel.
I, too, find myself upon a promontory,
not as you were on Ogygia, alone,
trying to break the blue distance with the naked
eye, but, high above the street, I look down
into the laps of strangers by the carful
rolling past one another at Main and Broadway,
where you, when you were young, ate lunch, shot pool.
Across Triangle Park, in the glass grid
of the Hyatt, travelers light the same lamp
over and over. Boys with half heads-of-hair
ride skateboards down recirculating fountains.
Here, you are already strange.

Under the sunset shifting and serene
you lie in an ancient town
sinking, lost as Troy.

Eleuthera

blue folds
waves

fall white
on the white beach
hissing
black weed
snakes

white stacks
cloud
the far sea
edge

the black man
drops his hammer

among the sharp
thick tongues
of foliage

looses his clothes
runs shining on the white
sand, kicking water

blue blossoms
lick his body

galloping
rising falling

eruptions of jet

Flood

Big Spring Park
February, 1991

In the wind of your mouth
I sucked a moon with a face
like the town clock.

In your darkness I drank
a black wine studded
with lax old berries.

On the muddy path
I find half a pencil
and think I'll write

these lines to you.
But, pulp to the lead,
it shatters. I fling

it on the water
with a curse: these
yellow shards, may

this cold swollen rock-
knocking stream hurl
them straight into
the bull's-eye of your heart.

Eros

Who are you?
In deepest night you come
into my bedroom wearing
your delicious boy's body.
I think of graying Sappho
crisscrossing the Aegean
searching for you
as you fled before her.
Bite by bite, my mouth
and body taste your pungency
sweet on the tongue
as salt and satisfaction.
On my black bed
our hungers eat away
our flesh, yours young,
mine not quite
old, until our bones
slide against each other
naked and unhinged,
as alike in this dark room
as seeds inside maracas.
This rattling of our bones:
a percussion, a music!
I sink into my sleep
again without a candle.

In the Darkness

The body asks its own questions.
My skin yearns toward yours.
My mind has folded itself like wings
into the egg and disappeared.

My flesh gorges, slacks, and translates
into flame, though it makes no sense
and is not real. I am tough-minded.

But at your touch my brain blooms
black red like the night inside
your mouth: a rose that never
goes to seed opens its petals furred
like pelts pulsing with dark blood.
Your tongue swells with what it cannot
utter, ancient utterings my tongue takes.

By the Sea: The Dream of the Body

To know what it wants.
Always to have what it wants,
like a spoiled baby, plump, luxuriant,
always the center of a circle of admirers.
No past, no future, just the zero
of this moment. One perfect day
on the island of Eleuthera
I, in my fifty-first year,
ride a bike along a bright
sun-dappled lane as if I were
a ten-year-old who thinks
somebody fifty nearly dead.
The air lifts my sweaty hair
and fills the cells that build
my skin. Gravity, inertia
curl in my wake.
Suddenly, through the vegetation,
I can see into the depths of sky
and blue, blue ocean. Flying
down this road tented
by the wind-bent casserinas,
I cannot see the end
of them. They stretch
beyond my death, beyond
the swelling, falling of the sea,
like breath; beyond the movement
of pine needles among each other,

like voices; beyond the tremblings
of live sky above them, like young
sex, when the body knows
each pore's single appetite.
The body is the island,
the garden. Our hunger is itself
the fruit (apples, mangoes, all
that is sweet and succulent)
that dangles into reach.
Oh stretch the suppleness
of every joining in your body
toward that fruit. Eat.
Make death, and undo it.

Epiphany, 1992

I went out into the frigid night
to shift cars in the driveway.
Finished I looked up into the clear
black distances of Orion hunting
in circles through the dark,
his leg thrown over the horizon.

If only I could empty myself
of you and your absence.

No. Then you would be lost
as if you'd never been
climbing the dark with the stars,
striding with your black dog
across the winter sky brilliant
because it is void and cold.

Janus

The mud of January,
cold ooze shining
out in the open rain
for ten straight dark days.

Under it the bodies of people
I have loved lie papery, unreal,
and bulbs that will be narcissus,
tulips, daffodils, hold their own
against rot and freezing.

Dirt. If I open the door
of my skin, there
it is, pulsing, glistening,
only itself, implacable.

The Whale

Purple, languid, content, cruising
the ocean bottom, land without light;
behemoth fueled by a cumulus shifting breath
rolled in its lungs delicious as smoke
in the addict's mouth, but having at last
to break the membrane of the surface to take
air. So while I peel potatoes, or bend
to switch the channel on the car radio, grief
may without warning break my face,
my everyday skin. Because there was
a summer day when the clouds overhead
like magic slates rewrote themselves in silence,
because the falling chatter of the chimney swifts
at twilight sank tighter and tighter into circles
of darkness, I know that the world does speak,
but in all its tongues each word means good-bye.

On a Perfect Day

. . . I eat an artichoke in front
of the Charles Street Laundromat
and watch the clouds bloom
into white flowers out of
the building across the way.
The bright air moves on my face
like the touch of someone who loves me.
Far overhead a dart-shaped plane softens
through membranes of vacancy. A ship,
riding the bright glissade of the Hudson, slips
past the end of the street. Colette's vagabond
says the sun belongs to the lizard
that warms in its light. I own these moments
when my skin like a drumhead stretches on the frame
of my bones, then swells, a bellows filled
with sacred breath seared by this flame,

this happiness.

A Glimpse

Just a glimpse down the side street
as I speed past on Maxwell.
In my vision no more than two
seconds: he and she
in a front yard. His arms,
wrapped as if around a trunk
he climbs, pull her up
to his mouth, his legs planted
in the grass on either
side of hers, unlike in
advertisements where
postures make a dance
of appetite. No.
Here he bends onto
her, and she, face open
and straight up, meets
him full on as if each
one has crossed a desert,
or lasted out a long, long drought.
One is rod, one is rock.
In their mouths, from
their tongues, spring waters.

In the Kroger: For Jim,
His Daughter Dead in a Wreck

Last night your beautiful child rose
into my sight as I looked from my window
at the blooming apple tree in moonlight.

Today at the store I came upon you
by the cereal shelf struck
like a monument, so hard and real
your bones shone like marble
or alabaster, bright arcs of grief.

Before the wreck when I saw you
with your cart, a different man
stood in your dark suit,
your everyday skin, that hide
we all wear. Now
you light the aisle.
Your bones, old moon slivers.

The Sudden Appearance of Love

Marco Island, Florida

The canal blackens under the sunset,
glitters with shards of fire
flung into mosaic on its moving skim.
Like tapestries unfurled from tableaux
of ruby clouds, the water tempts me
to step off the dock and walk.

Suddenly, out of the dark underwater
a fish, not big, not beautiful
(a mullet or a jack), leaps,
shattering viscosity
into scales of light, smacks
the air as with an open hand
showering iridescence
on the broken floor.
Circles widen into black horizons.

By Dark

Out of the blue
a black boomerang,
a gull's shadow
drops to the beach.
I walk at water's edge
as far as I can go
and still get home by dark.
Returning, I step
in my own footprints,
a new way back.

Aubade

At daybreak a crow's hard cry
breaks apart the darkness,
which disappears black
feather by black feather.

February 23, in the Cemetery

The first blue sky since December
today arches over me.
Late sun strikes the holly leaves,
waxy and burnished.
Two rabbits turn figure eights
among the tombstones.
Two sparrows tumble on the dead grass
in their mating flurry.
A crow as still as the stone of the urn
he stands on: the black triangle of his beak,
            the black star of his eye.

Exercise in the Cemetery

At dusk I walk up and down
among the rows of the dead.
What do the thoughts I think
have to do with another living being?
In the eastern sky, blue-green as a bird's egg,
a cloud with a neck like a goose
swims achingly toward the zenith.

Heike's Window at Nightfall, from Versailles Cemetery

Perhaps the dead can see in Heike's window
and, after dark at dinnertime, sit
upon their stones in rows mesmerized
as at a picture show, watching
through the narrow glass, slivers
of lives: Irwin's arm reaching
a jug of tea; Harck's boy arm extending
a cup that water fills; Heike
capping berries at the sink, then lifting out
the bread the toaster raises. These gestures
fascinate the dead who watch that glass
as unforgiving and as hard as molten sands
they've crossed. On my own path
falls the light from Heike's window,
a flattened, grave-shaped shining
I step into.

The Locust

 . . . is an ugly virgin
plain daughter
favorless and poor.
But when May comes
and birds sing wedding songs
the country shines, the locust blooms,
a white bride
vulgar with promise.

She roots in dirt.
From dirt she draws her ugliness
and spins the veil that covers
dirt that rises, branches
to this flowering of dirt
sweetening the air,
rounding the sky
with blossoms.

In the Moment of My Death:
For My Father

You were simple, I suppose,
delighted by life
so that sickness and death
came to you as a surprise
out of the shadows of your heart.

In the moment of my death
may your old happiness light my way,
and the image of your face
smiling, happy at my coming,
be a lantern in the dark.

Hungry Fire

for J.J.F., 1941–1990

Everything becomes fire, and from fire everything is born.
—Herakleitos

Home is where one starts from. As we grow older
The world becomes stranger, the pattern more complicated
Of dead and living. Not the intense moment
Isolated, with no before and after,
But a lifetime burning in every moment.
—T. S. Eliot, *Four Quartets*

The flames ate the house from the bottom up,
sought with their tongues around the chimney,
then devoured whole an order of place, time,
and generations: Sparta, Kentucky, 1990,
the infinite regression of mothers and fathers
from the single person, only child—
James Joiner Fielder, 49 years old the week before,
the age his father died. We predicted
the fire: he drank himself to sleep most nights,
after stoking to red heat his wood stove;
he baked tuna casserole from his own recipe
or fried steaks at three in the morning,
leaving the burner on, forgetting to eat;
the wiring, new in 1927, frayed, unraveled.
When his mother, Hope, died, he divided
himself in two and piece by piece gave all
her things away: the cut-glass punch bowl,
"before some bastard steals it," the pillow-

cases from her bed, embroidered by Aunt Molly:
"Go to Sleep like the Flowers"; her jewelry,
her clothes. His own things he kept,
though there was little room for him in the house.
He farmed as well as Pick, our grandfather,
better than his uncles. He knew where his ground
was rich. His big-leafed tobacco grew taller
than his neighbors' because he knew when rain
was coming and set his plants in time.
He loved machinery—the older, the more
useless, the better: the Case steam engine
Pick bought in 1919, the thresher from the thirties,
the metal-wheeled tractor from the twenties,
and the '42 Ford cattle truck, sunk to the rims
behind the barn, its cab grown full of ragweeds.
He spent his last afternoon on his John Deere,
pulling his brand-new wagon around and around
the two blocks of Sparta. The men at the store
shook their heads, laughed, admired the wagon.
He always wanted Hope to watch him. If he went
to Southern States in Winchester to buy a part
he'd call her twice, at least, before returning.
And twice during the year of her small strokes
she came downstairs in the morning to find
a Sparta boy in his bed on the side porch.
She asked her cousin once, a worldly man
in from the army, "Can you tell me exactly
what a homosexual is and if I know any?"
As they looked out over the long lawn
toward the draw-chain gate, he answered, "No,"

she knew none. But with all this,
the fire still stunned us, a catastrophe
unthinkable, yet simply an explosion
into the present moment of the workings
of the years, the entropy of this peculiar order.

But in this house the order, though old,
was fresh still, undiscovered and guarded
by his ownership: in the parlor secretary
the letters to Pick about his sons' drinking
and cockfighting, from wise Dr. Lovell
who birthed them all; in the dining-room
press the twelve tin cups of the picnic set
that went to Boone's Creek on Sundays;
Lily's iron skillets and pots on wide shelves
in the back-porch pantry, among the ranks
of canning jars; the packet of blue-backed deeds
in the desk under the front stairs tracing
the ownerships and boundaries of seven farms
Pick gave his sanity and strongest years
to getting for his children; the stack
of unquilted quilt tops Lily made from pieces
of their worn-out best ("Something from nothing,"
she always said); all the lacework, the fine-
stitched nightgowns and petticoats laid
in tissue in the cedar chest Uncle Walter built
in the penitentiary; the black pages
of photographs, some the only remnant of faces
once as familiar as our own in the mirror—
all broken, rendered into elements,

inchoate ashes, by those bright tongues
that made each room a hell to bring
the house down into its own foundations.
It settled finally into the rock hole that held it up
and defined those spaces where we walked in air,
those lifted rooms that held our lives' beginnings.

At first it hissed. It could have been put out then.
Then it crackled as it fueled past return, then
it sang and roared in the destruction
that he required of his sin, depriving us
(heirs, too, as he was) of secrets written
in the secret order of this house. He blamed
us for our impotence to save him from sodomy
there on the dining-room floor
under the watchful faces of Hope's Haviland
looking down from their places in the cupboard.
Before he passed out loathing himself, he paid
Randy Perkins, already having forgotten the wave,
the irresistible wave of desire that rolled over
him always unexpectedly, carrying him away
from himself, away from the order Hope left
him in the hope that it could save him.

As Virgil writes, "Gods of my country!
I follow, and where you lead there I shall be!
Preserve my house, preserve my little grandson! . . .
                    And now we heard the roar
Of the fire grow louder and louder through the town
And the waves of heat rolled nearer ever nearer."

On that first springlike day, smoke and heat
still wavered into the clear March sky
from the hopscotch of rubble I prodded through:
a stack of pink-flowered saucers melted together;
the blackened shards of the meat platter; a few
orange and blue flowers of the Chinese tea set
that stood in its tray on the sideboard
the eight years since Hope died;
the blue enamel tea kettle filled with water
from the firemen's hoses, still in its spot
inside the kitchen fireplace; the nested
tablespoons fused, rusted, their silver gone;
his brand-new typewriter, the keyboard
bones of flimsy fingers warped by heat.
This is ruin, what comes of siege, invasion:
not one stone left upon another. Shining
towers, broad streets: the eastern windows
that caught the morning sun and threw it back
to travelers on the road; the cool, generous
hall where the spiral stairs lifted; the parlor
where sunlight pooled through the bay window
onto the bright garden of the old carpet.
The company-best of that room dismantled
by the quick ferocity of flames:
Pick's life-size portrait, heavy in gold leaf,
hanging beside the framed papers of Thunder,
his Walker foxhound. Twisted metal, the stem
of the organ lamp, its globed roses exploded,
marks their places. The books stood in the shelf
as the glass shattered in front of them: *The Royal*

Road to Romance, Songs That Never Die, the volumes
of *The American Educator,* the Bible where Lily
recorded in her veiny script births, marriages,
deaths, the time of day, the dates, the years.
The coffin-shaped Steinway, its legs thick
as elephants', all its strings snapped, tangled
in the cellar hole, collapsed into the pit.

Prodding with the bent poker he used last night
to stir his logs, I lifted and turned all the pieces
I could move, searching for whatever might remain,
for something left intact that might raise the house
again, reorder in their orbits the scattered atoms
that made the pattern here. I longed to find
Harmonia's necklace, the one beautiful thing
intact, a miracle of survival in the ruins
from which could be drawn all that was lost at Thebes
fractal of the wholeness here dissolved:
the circle of talk around the bedroom fireplace
winter nights; the talk of women, white and black,
shelling peas for canning on a summer morning;
Lily singing "Amazing Grace," thinking of a grave
at Black's Station while she ironed; he, Johnnie,
and I at hide-and-seek, racing out into the cold
rooms from the safe hub of women at the hearth:
"A bushel of wheat, a bushel of rye,
all not ready, holler I!"

Finally in the white ash of the kitchen
the firemen at daylight uncovered his

body curled in its first posture
on the floor beside the oven. Nearby
I pried up the overturned sink cabinet
and found, still in the wire drainer,
his supper plate, without a chip or smudge,
of the blue-willow set Lily bought in 1917,
as noted in her diary, from a traveling salesman.
He washed his plate and fork, perhaps his last
act of order, put Silly and Marie, his dogs, outside
to safety, perhaps as Randy, needing money,
was walking in the kitchen door.

On my shelf of blue glass, the plate now stands
indistinguishable except to those who may see
in it a blaze of balance, of wholeness,
a family rooted in a place of dusty paths,
dirt roads with grass down the middle, of barns,
gardens, neighbors, cattle, itself a miraculous
duration, itself rare, not its loss. For in that plate's
round continence, three small blue men among blue
trees, flowers, houses, cross a blue bridge
toward the sea, toward distant mountains, a comfort.
Deep in its scene, far beneath its glaze,
on the other side of the world in fact, stands
a white house. Its windows catch the morning
sun among green trees where guineas will clatter
themselves to sleep in the long peaceful fire of sunset.

Portrait of the Artist as a White Pig
(2006)

Life in this world is full of pain. But pain, which is the contrary of pleasure, is not necessarily the contrary of happiness or joy

—Thomas Merton, *Seeds of Contemplation*

. . . he who kisses the joy as it flies
lives in eternity's sunrise.

—William Blake, *Several Questions Answered*

I

A Human House

To have a task that takes you
below ground to the basement,
feeling your legs spring under
you as you descend the steps
to pull the shirts, dry, off
the clothesline by the furnace.
Then to fold them, and the towels,
and ascend through the rooms
of the house, with the perfume
of cleanliness rising
in your nose. To see sunlight
falling on the rug of the upstairs
hall, to feel the June air
move across the bedroom
as if you walked in the head
of a tree. To climb
to the attic closet carrying
winter clothes, wool scratching
your arms. To fling open
the windows to release
the stale air. Then to sit
in your chair on the porch,
reading maybe, or writing a letter
you've owed for months;
to watch the shifting sky
through the thinning branches
of the yellowwood tree.
All day to inhabit!

Like a fox in her den,
a bird in a knothole,
an ant in its tunnel,
I belong here. My house
is as real in the world
as water or air,
as the birds' clear vowels
that rise through fading
light at the day's end.
And then, after night falls,
to stand in the dark backyard
looking into the golden light
of the rooms you inhabit
in the house that is your
body's body, and to see
on the kitchen table
the voluptuous wine
in the dark mysterious bottle
which you at supper all but emptied.

The Concept of Morning

But what interests me here is the specific mystery of sleep partaken of for itself alone, the inevitable plunge risked each night by the naked man, solitary and unarmed, into an ocean where everything changes, the colors, the densities, and even the rhythm of breathing, and where we meet the dead.

—*Marguerite Yourcenar,* Memoirs of Hadrian

I arise from the grave of the bed.
I re-muscle from the lapse into nothingness.
I put the self back on like a shirt.
I re-affix my face. I crack the egg
of the closed eye.

I open my eyes to light, to its comforting
habits of color, of patterns in the rug,
in the flowers on the drapes, in the sunlit
veneer of my dresser, in the shifting
leaves outside my window. These shapes
enfold me like a second mother's arms.

I am retold out of the gibberish of the night,
composed again from the junk of dreams,
from the chaos of the blood drumming
in the veins like a river running
toward the night when we cease being:
practicing, practicing.

Roofer

I

He squats, sticky as a fly on the roof's
steep pitch. It's all in the angle
of his feet to his ankles, in the bend
of his knees. Loose-jointed as a dancer,
he sits tight, tilting his head
this way, then that to see the shingle
fitted straight. He doesn't touch
the cigarette that trues itself, dangling
from his lips.

I've come awake this January morning to the sound
of crowbars wrenching at my neighbor's garage,
to the crack of hammers, methodic, knowing.
Nothing frantic in these sounds as old as shelter,
as familiar. I see him stand, jointlessly unfolding,
pull from the holster on his hip the shingle knife,
as easy as you'd pluck the fork beside your plate.
From my second-story window, I see him walk
along the sky edge into the crooked arms
of the apple tree. On his khaki shorts
I see black patterns of his scooting.

At home among the highest branches, he stands,
bone relaxed, muscle lapsed, arms akimbo,
and talks to his partner on the ground.
I see their words, their laughs, but cannot

hear them. Into a green wheelbarrow, his cohort
loads the flung-off shingles, while,
at the zenith, the roofer, on his haunches now,
begins to cut, like feather into wing, each
outer shingle to its edge, its proper place.
At the lower corner, he balances one leg
out upon the air as comfortably
as if it rested on a hassock.

II

By the end of this short winter day, there
have been at least three weathers: a sudden
drenching shower; then windy, cutting sunshine;
and now dark cold closes in. The roofer hauls
his hand under the sparse lift of his hair.

The woman of the house, her arms around themselves,
steps out to chat him up about the job.
They pantomime. He smokes, hammers, too,
in the same deft rhythm, positions the nail.
With one stroke, it is home. He stands
again, two-handed, reaches in his apron pocket
languorously as if to scratch himself.
His foot slips at the corner as he talks
and smokes and turns to shift. No bother. Only
start the move again. He cuts and flings
the trimmed-off pieces in a careful heap beside
the woman. He stands, oblivious to wind
and coming dark, to look at what is done
and what remains to be done.

Desire

My cat in the sill,
hunched mean as a fist,
steely as a coiled spring,
studies a foolishness of sparrows
in the tree outside the window.
A pounce in check, she holds
her ears erect like wings of bats
that sail out upon the air
buoyant with what they hunger
to snap up, rend, pulverize,
swallow into the lustful
muscle of such flight.

From My Attic Window

I see the roofs of neighbors' houses,
and the muscle of a bird's back as it flies
into the red ribs of sunset
beyond the courthouse clock.

All that sideways light
gilds the familiar, singes
the dark spine of the yellowwood
in my backyard, my sway-backed garage,
the house next door,
and lays long black shadow out
behind them like an overleaf.

Across the field
that I can only see the edge of
shines my mother's window
(another face behind it now),
from which she watched
each night darkening the world.

Among the Stations of the Cross on the Grounds of Taylor Manor Nursing Home

After a long winter and a cold March comes the first warm day.
Under the mild sky a farmer in the next field calls his cattle.
"Ho-up," he sings out of his belly, and from under the bill of his cap.
Doves hoo their cries of love; robins' declarations fill the air.
The cows, rough in their winter fur, saunter sedately spaced
into sight. After them, the haunchy calves tumble through the gate,
then the wandery newborns. I stand among the Stations of the Cross,
amid the Sisters of St. Joseph buried in a circle. "Lord, help me
to bear the partings that must come," says the stone I stand beside.
I turn to face the nursing home and the flowery hill where
my demented mother once scourged every dandelion.
The wind's small breath implies sweet grassy dung.
A crow, still stubby-tailed, stands on one foot, then
the other, on the top branch of a tall, bare tree.

Waking Up, in May

The bass of the thunder
rises beyond the locusts,
under the hill. Closer,
another voice answers.
The knowing grackle
trills its three-notes,
moves here, there
among expectant leaves.
Then rain begins,
taps out rhythms,
rolls its slurred notes down
the roof. Thirsty grass
opens its mouths, and tight,
new gardens breathe, unfurl
beneath the drumming torrents.

The quick baton
of lightning!

In downspouts and gutters,
rapturous phrasings,
downpouring streams.

Riddle

Made of movement, but moving nothing
in order to move, I ride myself
through the grass. No warmth of my own,
I depend on the sun. Always as wary
as you are, I fear the cold wind,
the sun behind the clouds, and darkness
that lasts so long I must hole up
below-ground bound in circles
of myself and sleep the winter out. But now
June sun heats the garden path, and singes
the pillow of rock on which the sundial sits.
All morning, over the top of your book
you spy me flashing like a needle
along your vision's hem, stitching
light to shadow, sage to thyme.
Eye-quick, you see not me but zigzag
trembling of the yarrow, until I levitate
into the narrowness beneath the sundial.

By noon, my oven's fiery, and I,
near melting, pour out into the ivy
bordering the garden. Air shimmies
above the bricks, and I, disinhibited
by heat I've drunk so recklessly,
just drop myself in loops, heedless
of the gardener with his hoes
and other handles passing back
and forth about his work.

Then I'm gone—my notice sudden is.
It bothers you to lose my place.
Furtively, in golden light you rise,
fold your book, and as you walk inside
are stopped—a tighter breathing!
There am I risen, too,
toward the sun, on the closest log
of the woodpile, my spotted shaft
draped artfully in camouflage
among the pulp. My lidless eyes
proclaim me to you as I am, as what
you see but cannot know: the bright
black bead of zero in my gaze
unblinking at the dark, the cold.

What am I?

The News

Nothing is gladder than morning:
sunshine fallen like new pennies
through the backyard trees. All the sounds
of beginning: crows warring overhead,
children shouting on their way to school,
cars accelerating, carrying people to work.
The flame of impatiens out my kitchen window,
the cat, hungry, nipping my ankles,
the slap of my neighbor's screen door
as she returns her face to the sky,
then bends to pick up the news of this day.

Diana, of a Certain Age, Takes a Bath

My body is drifting out of its familiar shape
like a great, slow cloud in August.
My muscled calves deflate,
my cheekline sags,
my waist fattens.
After the chase
I still enjoy my bath, the luxury
of perfume on my breasts,
my neck, my thighs,
as Nofretete did, or Cleopatra,
just as in my salad days.

But sometimes in the mornings now,
fresh from sleep, I skin off
my gown before the mirror
and the girl I used to be,
my flawless pearly body,
suddenly appears to me,
rises tranquil as the moon
gliding out of clouds,
and strikes me breathless
as at the forest pool
when I spied Actaeon in his blind
(his arrows useless in his quiver),
drinking in new quarry:

the shining of my body,
fulsome and deadly as his hunter's eye.

Terrified as the deer I turned him into,
I, too, am dogged by what I know is coming.

The Song of the Furnace

In the mirror my lower face diminishes
when I smile, and a tissuey wrinkle deepens
under my eyes. I am almost old.
Am I brave enough to be alone?
In this moment, my furnace sings
all through the house its burden
of comfort. My body bent to
the shape of a question mark,
warms on my bed covered in fall sun.
My mind somersaults in an ecstasy
of near-sleep. Excepting the comma
of my cat, fitted to the hollow
of my arc, there is no creature
I think I need inside this peace.
A voice might cut
like the hard side of a hand
against the long throat
of this song.

Realty

Rows of new homes, tidy in plastic siding, come
creeping over the hill toward the clapboard house
collapsing into its center under its own weight,
its porch barely clinging, that was built to fit exactly
the farmer's rocker, the wife's churn, her canning table.

This bulldozed valley, pocked with manholes,
will not be dark again for eons, its trees uprooted
that broke the winter wind and made the summer shade,
that stood beneath the fixed stars the farmer watched.

By the truckload, window assemblies and doors in frames
daily arrive in the raw streets, while the house, its angles
all askew, falls into its own pit, a mouth hungry
as its fireplace where the windy tongues inflamed
the black throats of all the chimney chinks.

November

brings its own odd comforts,
mercury dropping,
gray all over:
the highway where I'm driving,
the sky clamped shut against the earth,
the earth itself.
Even the trees dissolve
into their own gray smoke

and long ago gray dusks,
when I lay on the scratchy rug
listening to the radio
while my mother hummed, filling
the rooms with supper smells,
and, on the blackening windows,
my breaths made a blistery skin
I could not see through.

Sam's Club in Winter

Freezers long as freight cars chock full of rock-
hard cakes, pies, lasagnas, plastic sacks of crucifers
(when I unseal a door, its breath resists and sighs).

Rows of hot, baked hens, taut with succulence.
Chicken breasts cradled in styrofoam, corded like firewood.

A spill of fresh fruits from the tropics and the underside
of earth: beguiling little crates of clementines, nubile
grapes in see-through plastic. A grove of greenery
and banks of flowers, each blossom netted against bruising;
shelves tall as trees, toilet tissue stacked up into darkness.

Outside, winter's first Alberta clipper nudges around
the corners of the big box, pokes the thin skin of plenty.

Hunting for a Christmas Tree After Dark

A sudden mildness in the cold field.
Scraps of snow still strewn on the hillside.
The net of stars cast out overhead.
The shapes of old cedars come toward me
familiar as loved bodies approaching
from a long way off.
The creek in a hurry, as full of itself
as a zipper, the slow-melting snow.

I can hardly make out the rock fence
wavering up the hill, cold stone
on cold stone, stacked together
by unknown hands so many years ago.

How grateful I am for this moment of peace
my body has made with gravity, this
pulling things out of their places
and holding them in,
like Orion the hunter, who, when I blink,
seems to throw his leg over the low fence
of the horizon and climb into this bound with me.

Up ahead, looking for the one perfect tree,
my cousin John. His lantern bobs through
the dark meadow. He raises the globe
of light over and over in prospect.
I hang back, feeling rich in the black
waste, safe in this bowl of earth,

with rocks outcropping in the flattened grass,
trees wet, dirt sweetened by the downhill run-off
of all fear. Though the Interstate throbs
and the town lights bleed into the blot
of circling trees, from here the stars redeem
the dark that makes them shine.

II

My Life Story

I stood in my crib. Dust floated in a shaft of light.
I splashed in a metal tub on a sunny porch.

The years took the mule barn, its mountains of hay,
its ladder to the loft, and columns of sun
where swam the sweet talcum of flyaway earth.

The years took my stringy body that scrabbled
up the ladder, that could bend in circles over
backwards, and turn itself in cartwheel
after cartwheel across the shady grass.

Eventually, the tall banks of August clouds
and fire tongues in the grate on winter nights
spoke to me of a new life,
promising richer days and nights to come.

The years took our house, cool and dark,
generous as a healthy heart, where in September
a cricket sang under the kitchen hearth.

They took my mother with her red hair
and her creamy skin, and my father
whose laughing head shone with the fire
of summer as he shoveled corn to his pigs.

When I awoke one day, my bloom
was past. Those who loved me first were dead,

and promises had blown away like chaff
or clouds, which dazzle now only in the moment
of their height and roll.
The years have given back the thing itself.

In the House with the Red Roof

I lie in my crib watching
dust drift through sunshine.
I see the pipe holding
the orange-hot stove
to the chimney bricks.
I see the shut white door
Mother clicked behind her
when she left
me. I hear a cricket
singing under the staircase
and the drone of an airplane
in the blue sky of the window.
Then I hear the ringing
of no sound at all, no sound
of her footsteps on the floor.

The Red Taffeta Dress

On Christmas Eve it was under the tree
in a long, flat box. My family's faces,
washed in colored light, turned on me.
I was afraid it was clothes.
But when I tore the tissue off
I loved the sight of it,
a dress as red as Sleeping Beauty's.

In Granny's cold bedroom, Mother pulled it
over my head. She'd sewn it right: it swept
the floor and framed my face to prettiness.
I walked out into the gazes of cousins,
aunts, uncles, grandparents, father.
How like a skin it was, wedding me
to the dream, a sure joining,
the red dress fitting my child body
like a lost piece in the puzzle of the world.

Their Bed

Tonight I go to sleep to thunder over the fields
and summer rainfall like my mother's voice
when she lay beside my father in their bed,
each of its posts heavy as a tree.
Rain dripped through trumpet vines
outside their open window.
I knew they pleased each other: he loved
her milky body, her hair like fire,
her fingers always doing. She loved
his wide laugh, his ease with cattle,
his biceps, hard as hedge balls,
that he squeezed in knots for us to feel.
In their bed they lay notched like forks
in the kitchen drawer. From my bed I heard
them talk about the rain—it brings on hay,
makes big tobacco leaves. Stiff with listening,
I hear what they heard (the fall of water,
heaving trees), and I drift away, carried
into the dark on swift currents of their comfort.

My Mother's Rooms

The rooms of Mother's house shone
with cleanliness and order. My father
lived there, too, but he and all
his habits, inside their house,
seemed also of my mother.
In her rooms, daylight was good
in every season. She read up
on architecture and situated
this last house on the hill's lap,
sheltered by the upward slope
and brightened by the falling
westward prospect in the front.
Then she planted trees: an ash
outside the kitchen window,
two hollies out the back, a stand
of pines along the fencerow,
with volunteer wild cherries up
and down. They grew tall,
but never close enough to darken.

The objects in her rooms gleamed
with careful choosing, and polish
from loved hands before her own.
The clock's voice, merry as a heartbeat,
circulated through the rooms.
Newly wed, my parents bought
the clock at auction at a death house
on Boone's Creek, where they also

got the coal hod that sat beneath
the mantel where the clock stood,
and a Currier and Ives in which a man
in a hat drew a bucket from a well.
Each piece, a bright stone set
just right, seemed to have grown
there in the green light, brighter
yet for her small resentment
of the weekly dusting.

These rooms were their backdrop
until their lives began to fray:
their cancers and dementia
quickened by a son broken
in a car wreck, a daughter
marrying contrary to her best,
one grandchild neglected,
another always sad—
they could not set things right.
Then came my father's sickbed,
skewed into the room
with the hod, the clock,
and the picture of the young man
at the well balancing the bucket,
always about to meet it, lip to lip.

Leaving the Shades Up

In the long twilights of November,
both evenings and mornings,
I like the shades up,
I like to see the gray world
looking in at my looking out.
I like to watch
the slow balancing of light
inside the house and out:
the shy stars returning,
becoming public, or fading
into the daylight sky
as when death came
to my father's eye.

Ultrasound

March 18, 2003

What trouble are you saved, small spirit?—
wavering there in the amniotic water,
scarcely realer than a dream
that bursts like a bubble in the morning light.

But you will never be abandoned to strangers
in a schoolroom, never venture, clutching
books and lunch, into the teeth of the world.
You won't know the flower of loss
when the buds of your breasts push at your shirt.
You are spared haphazards—
finding a work, a friend, a mate
whose demons don't inflame your own.
You will not end, my almost girl, where
your mother is, trying through acid tears
to divine the dark you rock in. Wrapped
in their black cocoon, your chromosomes,
your ventricles, your rank neural tube
echo the probings of the ultrasound.
The only answer is your mother's anguish.
Although you'll never swim into the world's
light, neither will your small, dark floating
bring you here: to joy's foreclosure
                    to such blind choosing.

Aubade

April 2, 2003

Awakening in the half-dark
I heard the lovely cry of a bird, six notes
over and over, moving farther and farther away,
like a seed never burst,
a bud never bloomed,
like a flag ever furled.
Then day broke all across the town,
and the first sun of morning
scored the roofs and eaves of houses.

To My Grandson, in the Womb,
on Washington Heights

I lie on my back in Kentucky summer grass,
my hat over my face, carried toward sleep
by the narcotic sunlight
and the cicadas' antiphonies.
In this bright little darkness
my eyes sting

picturing you cupped safely
in Lucy's belly, she in the sensible
shoes, since she snagged her high heel
and pitched to her knees in the street.
How strange you are,
hidden, distant, other,
carried on your own tide of blood,
grown from an egg into
the changeling the ultrasound reveals.

Here in this stillness, a mower
burrs on the next farm,
and in the lake a fish jumps.
But underneath your house the subway
rumbles like a troll, shaking already
the jelly of your bones.
Along for the ride, on weekday mornings
you board the "A" train for Times Square.
I fear for you in that pell-mell
as never for my daughters. Someday

an Agamemnon might summon you to arms;
enemies may fix you in their crosshairs, you
without even bones to speak of!
I pray that you will not be flung
from your proud city's heights, burst
like Hector's baby in the dust
beneath the walls of conquered Troy.

From this day-terror I am roused
by hoofbeats on the ground I lie upon.
I fling my hat aside and, dazzled by the sun,
make out a buck with half-grown antlers
dancing toward me; at my eruption
he turns to stone. The sunlight showers
around him. His dark eyes surge and deepen
before he rears, whirls, and rumbles back
into the shadows, parrying the sword of light.

Skating

Family: that mysterious collection of ghosts
           which, sooner or later, we become to each other;
           some, shades we never knew,
           others, shadows of those we loved the most.

                              —The Metaphysician's Dictionary

We move around the rink,
riding the waves of the organ's pulse,
under the sun of the spinning glory ball
showering particles of light alike upon
           the graceful dancers and the lame,
           who, limbs flailing, are carried
           willy-nilly against the flow,
           comical as the top-hatted man
           on the banana peel.

When the music slows, we
           stumble over the lip of the ice
           into the dark surround, out of
the cascading shards of light,
and, tipping our blades,
stagger toward a resting place, collapse,
looking back at our own, both gliders and duffers,
like pictures on black pages in an album.

Hidden there in the darkness,
we building, brick by brick,
a palace made of light,

where all is enfolded, a Heaven
      shaped like an egg
      where the skaters float
      uncertain and harmonious,
      like subatomic particles.

Your Company

for Aunt Mary
      (March 3, 1910–January 29, 2002)

Breathing to the rhythm of your breaths
(they cackle loudly in your throat),
no point to being here except being
here with you still being.
Such peaceful moments
when I sit beside the dying
whose lives have made my own.
You are here. I am here. For now, what else
is there? What is there to want except
the long ribbon of the past
scrolling to the end of itself?

Sitting with Aunt Mary
in Hospice

An eye that opens and then closes—
Such is the life that seems endless to thee.

—*Frithjof Shuon, "The Eye"*

My daughter sits beside your bed,
her fresh skin stretched full of herself,
her hair fanned on her shoulders, an aureole
under the hum of the fluorescent lamp.
On the bed, you are a husk from which
the seed has blown, your hair unruly
as old grass, your breath, a loud suspense,
and then another. Your eyes, part open,
clouded, still seem to see
me clearly. In them I see your wordless
grief and longing, and, astonished, see
my daughter in a body ruined as yours,
far past my care and comfort.
I accept that in an ever-nearer future
I will lie as you do, but I can't conceive
that her child's body, too, will
one day loosen on its rack of loss.
The river of days already carries me
off, but you and she are still borne up
out of this drowning on the flood
of my swelling, useless love.

The Reading Lamp

On Grandfather's eighty-eighth birthday
his children gave him a reading lamp,
which he trained on the newspaper
morning and evening. Sleek,
silver, modern, taller
than I was, it rose from the floor
on its leaden base. Its bulb
burned in the chromium shell
at the end of its gooseneck,
which my cousin and I bent
into snake shapes, scaring each other.

On the shell a gold sticker glistened,
embossed with a name,
a brand I can't remember.
Whom shall I ask?
Grandfather died the next year.
Aunt Grace died early of a stroke.
Aunt Mabel and Uncle Teddy,
of lung cancer. My father,
my mother, both gone. My cousin,
too—a suicide.

I alone have lived to tell this
little story, and now I approach
the dark to which they've gone.
A last hope, that lamp

still shines, like silver,
gold, a wondrous light
which won't yet yield its name.

Eating a Pear from the Tree My Father Planted Thirty-One Years Ago

For God so loved the world that he gave his only begotten son,
that whosoever believeth in him should . . . have everlasting life.

—*John 3:16*

One hand still on the shovel he's used
to plant in his garden this pear tree,
an apple, and a peach, he wanted his
picture taken with the three saplings,
his two grandchildren, and the shovel.
What is he seeing as he gazes proudly,
more at the children than the trees?
Granted he foresees this moment
when the tree's strong spine holds
up a universe of golden, tempting orbs,
now about to shower down
upon the earth. He sees, I hope, beyond
his cancer, beyond his sorrows
for his children, past the future hurts
of the babies with him there, to this
far-off fall with its unlikely bounty.
Though the peach and apple withered
(sometimes the fate of virtue),
this great floozy of a pear
outlived him, and the sprout
that touched his hip is now
at least ten times his height,
its limbs so thick
they could be trees themselves.

This year the summer started early
(no late frost), was cool throughout,
replete with rain, and now the fall
stays cool but long, with no hard frost.
The pears have formed at every nodule
on this tree, at every notch where, back
in May, outpourings of white flowers
foreshadowed this. For two months
now the windfall has been greater than
the usual whole yield, and still
they're falling in the fertile circle
underneath the tree, so hard and fast
they come that they have pulled down
three big branches, loaded still, upon
the ground. I hope he's seeing this
October day of sky electric blue,
the heft of this gold sunset light.
Perhaps he knows the earnest hearts,
and hard, brave growth of the two
children beside him there, shading
their eyes from the sun that fell
that day on their brown shoulders,
thrown back in pride that they
had helped him plant these trees.

He planted trees, so enacting
his love and deep connection
to the world. He had Mother take
this picture so that a moment of beginning
might persist. For my own part,

here alone where his garden used to be,
seeing the many bushels of pears still
clinging after many weeks, still falling
(though several neighbors have
pear jelly on their shelves), regarding
the broken elbows of the limbs
that couldn't hold such flourishing,
I see the perfect figure for his heart:
a pear that I pick up, not bruised
from its long fall, not broken open,
not yet a sweetmeat at this harvest feast,
not sipped at by drunken hornets,
or gorged upon by jays, not burrowed in
by bees, nor fed upon by sluggish snakes,
without bite marks of coons or possums,
but shining in its globular perfection,
so winsome in its rusty wholesomeness
that I take its rough skin to my lips
and crack its flesh upon my teeth.

One Summer in the Life of My Mother

I have Three Treasures which I hold fast and watch over
closely. The first is *Mercy.* The second is *Frugality.* The third
is *Not Daring to Be First in the World.* Because I am frugal,
therefore I can be generous. Because I dare not be first,
therefore I can be the chief of all vessels.

—Tao Teh Ching, *No. 67*

I came upon the book again when I was cleaning out
the desk where she paid bills and kept farm records:
a calendar book, four days to the double page,
where she logged the events of summer 1958,
before my high school senior year. She wrote
on June 22, "Dear Jane,—I'm going to try to write
in this book everything that happens at home
so you can read it when you're back from France."
It was the first time I'd been away so long.
She was forty-four, with amber hair
and creamy skin, and on October pages
in the back, after summer days had petered out,
she listed in neat columns all the calories she ate
for several weeks on her reducing diet,
always with dessert at lunch and supper.
The days she noted here for me
are like a string of crystal beads, each full of light,
one scarcely different from the rest. She worked
hard, but each day brought pleasures: June 23,
a Monday, always wash day: "Washed—
took Charlie to his baseball game (Rebels 10—
Senators [his team]—4). C.B. involved in barley.

Had supper at 8 o'clock—read magazine—
at home and early to bed." That one word *washed*
belies her single-handed hauling
of the spin-dryer from underneath the stairs,
the difficult attachment of the hoses to the faucets
in the kitchen sink, and the hanging of a half-dozen
heavy loads of shirts, jeans, underwear,
khakis, and bedclothes on the backyard line.
But then the pleasure of a baseball game, making
a little supper, reading *Collier's* in the easy chair,
and up to bed by ten, without need to accomplish
beyond the day, nor any worry for tomorrow.

Only phrases here and there admit of any feeling.
Two days after my departure she wrote: "Up at six
so C.B. could get to the barley. I did nothing today
but mess around and read. Mrs. Setzer called tonight
and said somebody's father in New York
went to the pier, and saw you board your ship.
I was *sure* glad to hear even indirectly.
It's a funny feeling to think about you out
on the ocean and not be able to know
if you are sick or well, happy or sad—"
But her writing was not shaded; rather was
a useful record of life lived within its limits,
an accounting she made to save for me
that summer's slow days in their flow.
Four or five nights a week they played rum,
six- or nine-card, or bridge, all for fun,
spiced by the modest sums they wagered.

They played with sisters and brothers-in-law,
with friends and cousins, who were also neighbors,
with Old Boy, my father's cousin, old enough
to be his father, who lived back in the fields
alone, a rich man, whose black pick-up was
ramshackle as he, his clothes held on with pins.
Mother kept a tally of how much she won:
Thursday June 26: "Raining—Richard came in
and talked to me till Charlie got up—made some
potato salad & cooked green beans—called
Miss Mary Farney and fixed her a box of quilt pieces.
C.B. went to town. Charlie went to work
with Richard and his father this afternoon.
Six-card rum at Mabel and Tom's. + $5.00."

The rightness of these days rings true, no sense
of over-doing, even on the big day, July Fourth:
"10:50 a.m. Dear Jane, I miss you. I have just
finished frying chicken, making lemonade
for our all-day picnic—just my family—Nice day—
talked and ate. Charlie built a pony cart. The Allisons
brought the pup back. Everyone gone by 9 p.m.—"
after the last Roman candle exploded from its bottle.

The next day, a Saturday, she checked rain
on the daily weather grid: "Cleaned up from the 4th—
Pony League picnic—real nice. Charlie didn't go
so we came home early. Mary and Dav, Mabel
and Tom, Old Boy played 6-card rum till 1 o'clock—
—50 cents." Only three times all summer long does

she mention television, and then it's always
"Watched the Reds game on tv tonight."

In the back of the book, on pages for addresses,
she listed and crossed off chores remaining
in her yearly house cleaning, top to bottom.
"Upstairs—wash windows and hang curtains
washroom. Downstairs—hall—wash woodwork,
clean lights, wax floor—" and so for all the rooms.
She'd learned industry from her mother, but her days
were pleasureful: along with work of meals
and house, time for reading, napping, baseball,
playing cards, eating out at Jerry's or at Smoot's.
Her days were rich with people. No society as such,
but ample daily comfort of connection, talking
with her mother and her sisters on the phone
("Hello, what are you doing?"), visiting neighbors,
the ritual banter at card tables in the evenings.
On Wednesday, July 9: "Jane's first letter from France
came this morning. She ate an artichoke
in Deauville. Dovie was here and we cleaned
the kitchen. Richard ate supper with us. Mrs. Livesay
called and told me about her letters from Jo Ann.
Hogs are better. Went to Mabel and Tom's tonight
and stayed till 12. Charlie B. won $11.00. Rain."
The last day of writing, she figured totals
for three months: "from May 3 to August 4,
6-card +$22.50—9-card +$105.80." Nobody
else kept track, knew how consistently she won,
or guessed how much she relished winning.

What does this add up to? Not a remarkable life,
by standards of achievement, but still a wonder
of easeful time, mid-span, her children half-grown,
moving in their own directions, I, the older,
even on another continent. Simple routines
of cooking that didn't seem a burden, the cycle
of wash days and cleaning house in company
with Dovie. She accommodated Daddy's
movements and farm work: feeding the hogs
after supper, going to the stockyards
every week, seeing to the barley and the hay,
his several daily stops at the crossroads store
in Athens, buying bread, picking up the evening paper.
There were sadnesses and trials,
but they were short and trivial in 1958:
the luckless Senators didn't win a single game
all summer, though Charlie got his hits.
And on the last page of the book she sketched
the floor plan of the house she wanted, new
and ordinary, still five years away, without
the twelve-foot ceilings of this lovely,
too-big house of the peaceful summer
that I missed, that she wrote down for me.
It was a Golden Age, but, as ages go,
scarcely there, tipping in the balance:
past were my father's chicken-fighting
days and all-night drinking binges.
She had told him after years of pleading
that if he left again he'd come back
to find her gone, but us still there for him

to raise. Yet to come were her own sorrows,
a list not long, not extraordinary:
her parents died as she of course expected,
Charlie's head was broken in a wreck,
a long, slow cancer took her Charlie B.,
her sister Mildred died suddenly, too early,
Charlie's wound festered in his children.

Her heart broke, cracked the dam that kept
her sorrow in. Her dementia came on
fast, flooding out 1958, along with all
her other seasons. But because she wrote
this book, that summer isn't gone.
Here and now I read between her penciled lines
her mother's hope that I, though still a child,
would know her in a future which she could not
guess, as she was that almost perfect summer,
when my absence just rehearsed the losses
yet to come, a moment in her life of the best
that we can hope for: bright as the burning
of a July day, warm as the light of amber hair,
brief and brilliant as the summer sky.

III

Portrait of the Artist as a White Pig

At sunset on a November day, the world unrolls
itself beside the Western Kentucky Parkway.
Gilded in sunlight, bronze as a baby shoe,
the dead leaves burn on the trees, red, gold,
black, spread rich as an Oriental rug.
Green flames of side-lit cedars burnish all.

Then, over the short horizon appears the hero,
alien as brontosaurus, strange,
but of a multitude: white pigs,
a field full, eating, all snouts
to the ground they've rooted up, plowed
like furrows in the cognac-colored light.
That earth should take the form of this
strange beast, should eat itself and shift
into this shape! The bows of their backs
gold-leafed: snout and mouth to golden earth,
as hungry as one breath for the next.
Unnatural as Midas' kingdom
in the sideways sun, what other
brutes could translate this
bright dirt? This heavy
light? These showers of gold?

At Pleasant Hill, Kentucky, in January

(Shaker Village, restored 1964)

A day so cold my car tires roll like rocks
along the road. In the fields, only the cedar
trees seem at home in the ice-bright air.
My garret room high in the East Family House
has two plain windows, the only decoration
on the walls. In the upper sash, a wan blue
January sky hazy with crystalline veils.

In the lower sash, a drift of furnace steam,
birds riding by like sentences across my thoughts.
A nuthatch and a flicker scour a locust
for whatever mites survive this cold.
A chickadee levitates branch to branch.
Ever-indignant crows voice their complaints.
And on the ground, no Shakers, but family
groups of sightseers: an antic roly-poly child,
grandfather in a Scottish cap, stolid
parents slung with cameras and packs,
grandmother picking her way upon the icy path.

Then the music of a train. I can see it
over the white humpback hills, through fencerows
of naked trees along the umber skyline. It
stitches in and out of sight, blasts its horn again
at High Bridge crossing the Kentucky River.

Small as toys, its coal cars crawl, straightforward
as shoelaces, toward Dix Dam.

A weekend visitor, I am at home
in this resurrected village, this frozen
countryside, in which my mother was a child
just beyond the far-off tracks, in Wilmore,
where her grandmother grew up, too,
on this home ground
where I've never spent a night before.

Once every place but home was foreign, but home now
widens, becomes stranger than I thought possible. Here
in Shakertown I sleep like a baby on its mother's lap.
From my gable window I see dawn come
across the rim of the horizon, an orange
gash through which new daylight pours.

Taking the Train from Maysville to New York

September 11, 2002

Leaving Versailles at 4 a.m., only a glint of light
in the east. The stars so quiet. One watching
above the gable of my house, close as in childhood.
On the drive to Maysville, just a handful of cars
on the country highways. Out the window I see
the gauze of the Milky Way unrolled across the sky.
The Dipper so clear, dot to dot. Orion lazy, low
to the horizon. Near Paris, the sheerest sliver
of the new moon raises the old above the trees.

Then on the train headed toward West Virginia,
running alongside the broad-bosomed Ohio,
the levee now gold in the rising sun,
farmsteads, entire cities of rolled hay,
power plants with smoke plumes blooming
into the pink sky, towns of vine-latticed houses
facing the tracks. Oh for the voice of Whitman
or Twain to catalog these visions of America
framed by the train window, much as they lay
150 years ago. Through the dappled
trees yellowed in sun, I see the mist, the lovely
breath of the Ohio rising in shafts, alive, inviting
rest, but my sleep-heavy eyes won't close out
the sun blazing its pathway on the river.

The rails sing a low, syncopated song.
The coach cradles me and rocks across small rivers
and large, past cornfields tasseled out, past
vine-wrapped barns, square bales of scrap metal
heaped beside the tracks outside of Ashland,
past two women visiting on a narrow plant-filled
porch, past the aquamarine geometries of backyard pools,
past herds of cattle, heads down, shadows humped,
indefinite, wrenching up the generosities of grass
far, far yet from the city once innocent of its riches,
its towering heights, which now knows, like its poor sisters
all across the earth, the fist out of the sky, the shock,
the fire, the smoke-choked darkness, and descent.

The Light at the End of the Tunnel

Is this a poem that should be written?
I stand looking out the back window
of the last car of the train.

It has emerged from the darkness
of the tunnel into blinding sunlight.
I watch the track inexorably narrow
into a straight line behind us, finally
disappearing into the black mouth
we've just come out of.
Smaller and smaller, the doorway of light
at the other end of the tunnel.

Utopia: An Idyll

Everyone in the Utopia Diner seems happy:

the regulars who, in the middle of the afternoon,
wander in; the Greek waiters standing at their posts
joshing each other, all in short-sleeved
white shirts and slick black ties; the proprietor
in his bright Polo, licking his thumb
behind the cash register, counting out
dollar bills to dishwashers and busboys
changing shifts. He dispenses money
with equanimity, just as he takes it in.
One waiter lines up all the ketchup bottles
and pours the almost empty into the almost
full, until each table has a fresh, new bottle.

In the booth next to mine, two teenage girls
(known to the younger waiters, who smilingly
bring them extra fries, refill their cokes)
lean toward each other, whispering, in their
low-cut jeans and high-cut shirts, the skin
of their hips and waists glowing against
the leather of the banquette. An old couple
of familiars, he in a Yankees cap, she with
a Greek sailor hat upon her too-bright auburn
hair, order carefully, negotiating a split
of the three-egg, two-waffle breakfast
available twenty-four seven.

My eggs arrive exactly as I want them,
scrambled hard, with two twists of bacon
crisp and overcooked. On this November day
my decaf with skim milk, poured over
and over into my never-empty cup,
is ichor in my veins in Utopia, the diner.

Rose Week in the Brooklyn Botanic Garden

And what is so rare as a day in June?
Then, if ever, come perfect days.
　　　　　　　　　—*James Russell Lowell*

A gull like a paper plane
sails high on a blue current
over the garden gate where
a rose drops its red vestments
into the bloody puddle of a birdbath.
The traffic soughs, then
hushes, growls again.
Overhead, a sky out of childhood—
the country of clouds real as continents.
The air, sweet as a blossom.

Under their tiny backpacks, schoolgirls
in skirts below their knees straggle
along the path behind their teacher
in her oxfords and her headscarf.
They look back open-mouthed
at the old woman scribbling on a pad
and sitting cross-legged on forbidden grass.

The roses, two days past their prime,
still yawn and flirt. They have
their moment, after all. This is
as real as death, this silkiness,

these many-colored petals,
curling at the lip. The brilliance
of the Pearly Gates! The scent
of crimson at Life's Fountain!
Oh how sheer the Angel Tears!
The jumbo Grand Hotel entwined
with sunny Dainty Bess! At the bottom
of the garden, the purple thunder
roll of Distant Drums!

In the reflecting pool, two dragonflies doubled
careen in tandem like fighter jets refueling.
In Cherry Lane, a young mother, still egg-bellied,
drops on all fours beside her infant lying
on its stomach in the grass. Crisp in white
the baby spasms like a beached fish,
and the mother laughs her delight, all teeth,
inches from the baby's velvet face.

On the Eve of War with Iraq

March 17, 2003

Safe at home today, making my rounds
to the grocery, my office, the cleaners,
reading, preparing classes for tomorrow,
I think of those on the other side of the world
who might not be alive tomorrow—
boys and girls the age of those I teach,
costumed in camouflage and khaki,
ranged at the borders with gas masks and guns.

And in Iraqi villages and cities, fathers,
sons, grandmothers, mothers, soldiers
ply their routines at home,
getting their children dressed and fed,
laying in food and water, boarding windows,
cleaning weapons, awaiting the attack
the others poise for.

Perhaps Heaven is earth
without the water of blood,
air without the song of breath,
for every heart clutches at its own blood.
We know the fire will fall—we hope
on someone else, on someone else's
children, someone else's house—out
of the blank sky, the blind eye of the sun.

My Two Daughters in Paris

What pleasure it gives me to think of them
walking the leafy streets, the sunny quais, arm in arm
along the generous boulevards, looking for the right
table under the trees for a drink, or their supper.

I see them in les Jardins du Luxembourg looking
into the cool length of the Medici Fountain, then
on the gravelly terrace, their backs to the shadows
of the grove. They sit close under the stony gazes
of les reines de la France. In the distance, along
the pool's shimmer, their remnant childhood
dreams unfurl in patches of bright flowers.

The best of what they have from me is their being
in this tapestry, no forgotten pins, needles biting
through the fabric, as in the mother spell I weave.

When finally we say good-bye, whether I'm the traveler
or they, unthinkably, are leaving me, this temptation
I will cling to: the vision of two sisters in a garden,
the music of a strange tongue in their mouths, sun
gilding their hair, each head inclined toward the other,
hearts blooming, yearning toward all the earth holds out.

Nike of Samothrace

All victory is winged. Goddess, you
lean forward from the prow of your ship,
the folds of your chiton swept back
by the wind you ride upon at the top
of the main stairway in the Louvre.
You took this form in a lost town
on an Aegean island where husbands
gossiped and bartered in the agora,
and wives busied themselves in the dark rooms
of their houses, hearing the slap of men's
feet on the paving stones. Near the harbor
in a work-shed veiled in dust, you rose up
plane by plane, in the mind's eye
of a stonecutter, who, over years,
laboriously discovered you, chip
by chip, inside the body of a stone.

When at last he finished nicking, filing,
polishing, giving you the final caresses
of shapeliness, could he remember, any more
than we, the victory you commemorate?
For now you are Victory, the ache
of exultation, no sooner felt than gone.

You bear into the wind always
your wings of stone
spread to catch the lift of air.
And deep in your rocky bones

a Thracian breeze still blows,
exciting your fleshy nipple
under the wind-sheered cloth.
Tides of people swell around
the bow of your broken ship.
The lightning of their cameras
fixes you time and again
in the chiffon of winning. Your torso,
robust as the sea wind pushing you,
torques against all that is fleet.
You stretch back against these currents
the feathery stone of your resisting wings.

Les Jardins du Luxembourg

In the vista of the Queens of France we sit.
The fountains spill
onto the pools green, moving mirror.
On the terrace, the rows of plane trees
burgeon in the sun.
The palm fronds agitate
as in a tropic breeze.
Within the grove, the shadow opens
a dark inviting room
into which a runner disappears,
and a woman pushing a blue stroller,
and two young men bent forward from their backpacks,
and an old man with a newspaper under his arm.

A gardener with bronze legs
bends, trims the border of a border.

Leaving the Sidewalk Café

Overhead, crows squabble and parry
as I walk away from the restaurant where
glad voices rise and fall, riding the surf
of syntax, sentences in counterpoint
to sentences, cresting as they would have
to the ears of a Minoan lady pausing
on the Great Staircase to listen to
the cadences of talk at the banquet
she had left, or to a Neolithic woman
stopped in the cave mouth to hear her clan
feasting on a lull around the nightly fire.

I look back at the awning strung
with lights, and hear the sharp tattoos
of forks and knives against the plates.
No great occasion, only friends
in company eating together, all safe
for now from perils (the lightning strike,
the wind's maw, the worm of poison)
and threats (the loved body stiff as a claw),
while abiding harmonies of conversation
over food rise into the evening air
amid the ancient discords of the crows.

Portrait of Sue Richards
as a Young Girl

> Because it was a woman
> Who built a house for death
> A shining girl tore it down.
> —*Hildegard of Bingen*

See her now as she was then,
in the over-ripe Eden of central Florida,
a girl of eight or nine, skinny, tanned,
flint-eyed, shinnying up the tree, limb
over limb, as if there were stair steps
among the leathery leaves of the magnolia.
Slaphappy, giddy with daring, hell-bent
on the fiery fruit at the tip of a branch,
she doffs and bobs above the innocents
below, faces upturned, mouths agape.
"The world tree is blossoming. Two
realms become one. . . .
Never was leaf so green . . .,"
never so white the last bloom
she passes on her way,
fragrant as the queen's perfume,
purest vessel, round as a plate,
luminous as the moon.
She stops and meets the flower
lip to lip, drunk
on the glory of high heaven.

The Clouds, My Mother

Windermere Island, Eleuthera, the Bahamas

The white clouds on the horizon
billow against the blaze of sky.
Out on the water, I see the manes
of the breakers, then the clear aquamarine
where we swim, and beyond the reef
the black water where the barracuda,
amberjack, and tuna live in their imageless
world. On shore, the rapiers of palmetto
fronds under the morning sun,
the pastel houses set in dunes,
and, in the sand, footprints
of a cat and her four kittens, hieroglyphs
of a language lost in this sea place.
Almost unseen at home, the clouds
here fill the eye in their entirety, schooners
swelling, making for the verge.

Watching Stars

Eleuthera juts like an elbow
from the dark sea.
We lie on the warm sand
and watch for falling stars.
And what is one, or two,
or three, among the countless
brilliants that we see?
And yet their light is black.
I cannot see my hand
six inches from my eyes.

Behind us in the foliage
chameleons have turned black.
They flick from frond to frond,
and climb the spines of leaves.
Light years ago, these lights
we see tonight were buried
in the stars, and the sly lizards
with their lidless eyes
and traceries of bone bore
the weight of tyrannosaur.

Parable of the Reverse Sunset

We sit transfixed in the dusk, as if chained
in our chairs, the fire behind us, looking
at the eastern sky for the whole half-hour of sunset,
watching the sea and clouds shift, reflections
of each other. Patterns of light glisten,
tumble together (pink, red, lavender,
purple, black) like pieces in a kaleidoscope.
In the clouds we see shapes: a cat's head, a horsefly,
the outline of Kentucky, a baby sucking its thumb.
With all the pleasure of vacancy, far from our cares,
we watch this strangeness as if we might learn
something useful from such slantwise vigilance
(the luxury of looking where the action isn't),
something the direct, revolutionary Plato didn't.

First Kiss

We said good-bye standing at my car.
Your tongue was sly as an inside joke.

When I wiped my lipstick off your lips,
my fingers read the Braille of my longing,
an old alphabet, signs of a lost language.

April in Your Garden

The day falls open out of the sky.
Even the cedar bent from the wet late snow
seems to rise up into it
like the richest voice in a chorus.

Your body is as real as a tree.
I sit outside in bright sunshine
and see your movements tap like a ghost
behind the screen of the open window.

My hand gripping this pen
suddenly yearns toward home: between
your neck and shoulder, inside
the glove of your hand—places right

as the purse of the oriole's nest
I see rising, falling on invisible
currents high in the ash tree,
among green fists of new leaves.

Nearby

I doze on a bench in a garden.
Like a cat, I absorb June sunshine.
A bird dips so close I hear its bony
whir. My eyes open a slit. A butterfly
sips at a bloom that bobs under the tissue
of its wings. In the flowery light
my open book warms on my chest. A cardinal
pours out the syrup of its song. The pinks
throb in the still-cool air. A bee
forces the nod from a head of clover.
I sit up then, and see
nearby on the meadow grass
a hawk's shadow sailing in circles.

By Your Small Lake

At dusk I sit in the leftover sunshine
your dock absorbed this July day.
The gray boards, familiar as an old
blanket, practical as a spoon,
bring to mind your hands: warm, dry,
wise as a toolbox. The bourbon
you brought me smolders in my throat
sharpens my focus on a tableau
across the lake: many turtles, one
upon the other, heaped like rocks
on a tree trunk fallen
in the water off the far bank.
In the shallows near my feet, a carp,
cross-hatched, thick as a club,
whips to the surface for an insect,
breaks the dark back of the green
mirror, raising a chocolate cloud
from the lake's bottom. Startled,
an invisible frog grumps once
and, through the blackening surface, drops
like the pancakes your deft hands turned
this morning as you made breakfast—
your hands which wavered all night
over the lake of my body, its dark
mirroring our hungers rising
cunning as the turtles, shining
as the fish, to feed.

At Harmony Landing

> I never had a patient who spent part of
> his day looking over water.
> —*Sigmund Freud*

I am reading on the porch above the lake.
Cicadas are singing.
Now and again a breeze stirs the air.
I lift my eyes from my story,
and see, on the green water, circles
running outward from a center.

Immersed in words again, I hear a cry
or a double splash, or a thump
against the barrels of the dock,
but I never catch the fish
in air, the bird mid-dive,
or see the frog jump.

Still, the rings widen
into calm, their center fathomless.

Penelope's Night Out

Last night the fall crescent drifted down a summer sky.
The crickets sang their eternal one-note chorus.
You and I went to a party in a lovely room filled
with likenesses of the hosts in the beauty
of their youth, and with the books they cherish.
The room opened to a porch that gave upon a woods.
I watched its stand of handsome tree trunks fade
in the twilight. I chatted up a temptress in whose thrall
you once were held. After we drained the sweet liquor
from the last cubes in our glasses, we said good-bye
to friends, and to the pleasant new acquaintances.

We stepped into a moonless darkness and drove,
companionably touching hands, thighs in the golden light
of the dashboard. At home, we stepped out of our clothes
and laughed again at a conversation I had overheard.
We spoke, too, of Calypso's presence there. Then
as we lay beside each other, sleepily touching, with our
mouths, our fingers, our viscous skin, a wakefulness
surprised us like a wave, rolled us into the ecstasy
of this unlikely night, and dropped us, sleeping
soundly as you did, Odysseus, surrounded by all
your treasure, on the strange shore of home.

Sleeping with You

We climb onto the motorcycle of sleep.
I flatten myself against your back,
lock one arm around your waist,
and off we roar toward the rallies of night,
the marks of all our years streaming behind
us, like my white silk scarf rippling, useless,
riding the black wind.

The Traveler

I

A mile above the bony reach of trees, I doze
in a silver capsule skimming peaks of clouds.
The tiny egg of comfort I have swallowed
suspends my phobias, and, happy
as a baby on its mother's shoulder, lulled
by the uplift of the engines,
I come face to face with what I own and am,
with what I'm all but ready to surrender:

if all happinesses are not mine,
well, neither are all the sorrows.

Then, my adenoidal flutter jerks me
awake, saliva on my chin.
My furtive eyes open straight into the gaze
of the matron in Italian shoes across the aisle.

II

The joy of my face nicked by winter wind;
the joy of my legs, each swinging one foot
in front of the other on the dark sidewalk;
the joy of my eyes feasting on spun sugar
clouds afloat with the half-moon
above the towers of the glittering city;

the joy of my shoulders weighed down
by my packages and bag of books:

how few of us are lucky enough to live
the life were prepared for,

even for moments at a time, not deploying
the divisions of our body into foreign struggles,
but fitting our life like moss fits the trees
the plane passed over at such improbable heights.

The Chain: A True Account

(Mary House Gentry 1870–1952)

Mary seldom smiled, except to laugh,
and usually to herself, on dappled porches
where she sat all summer making something
from nothing, fancywork quilts from feed sacks
and old georgette; aprons from worn-out dresses;
doorway chains from empty thread spools;
socks she'd knitted long ago, she darned
now for the third time, or the fourth.
Such thrift was what was left of her religion.
As she worked, she sang like a cat purrs,
from underneath her throat, "Amazing Grace,"
"She Was Only a Bird in a Gilded Cage,"
or "Arkansas Traveler," all the verses
Uncle George brought back from Oregon.
Her eyes lifted sometimes, empty,
from her sewing. Her voice still singing,
she lost herself in shifting puzzles
of the light. She'd loved her mother, Martha,
dead at fifty-two, beneath the burden
of her husband's restlessness; Mary mourned
Paulina, oldest sister, tubercular at twenty;
and sickly Hiram, sweetest baby, dead
at eight, and as she stitched there on the porch,
her body felt the heaviness of walking through
the clinging grasses of the summer field
toward the shady rock-walled graveyard

at White's Station where her dead lie now
so far from home listening, she thinks,
for the whistle of the selfsame train that brought
them hopeful, seeking, from the mountains.

Or she laughed telling her husband Pick again,
or a sister, or one of her seven children,
a puzzle or a joke enjoyed many times before,
old stories of people they had known,
or known about, being strong or weak
or foolish, back in the mountains
or at White's Station, where they were
strangers for the first time in their lives.
Her favorite story was on herself.
In 1916 an earnest drummer found her full
of pride in her new house, its dining room
so big that all the children sat with her
and Pick around the claw-foot table.
So handsome the peddler selling dishes—
a big Blue Willow platter caught her eye.
It was unbreakable, he said, was more
than worth the seven dollars he was asking.
How it matched her Sunday dishes! Over
and over he let it fall, and it stayed whole
as a silver dollar, while in its glaze shone
the three Chinamen always crossing
the bridge; it easily would hold the meat
of four fried chickens. But the tobacco crop
was only just now set, the Prewitt Place's
mortgage soon was due. She always saved

her egg and cream money for the children's
new school shoes. But finally, she pulled
the jam jar off the back shelf in the pantry,
and bought herself a brand-new egg-shaped
platter tied with twine in its own box.
At suppertime her family filled their plates,
and she brought out the big surprise she'd promised.
The children held their breath, were saucer-eyed
at the huge blue-pictured oval of it.
"This platter will not break," she swore to them,
"no matter how it falls." She dropped it then.
It shattered in an awful silence.
One stunned second, and she commenced to laugh
until hard tears flowed down her face. Teddy
set up a wail among the solemn children.
"Pride goeth before a fall," she said
through laughter. Long after, for her
and for her children, that plate remained
the emblem of the danger of desire.
At three o'clock on those long summer days
she took her basket and her needlework
into the dark, cool hallway, where she sat,
head bowed before the console radio,
and soared and wept with "Stella Dallas"
till time to feed the hens and gather eggs.

In 1900 when they married, Pick was forty.
Old maid at thirty, Mary had already lived
another life, not the eldest daughter,
but the smartest and the prettiest, born

on Rockcastle River in Kentucky mountains
that hemmed her father in, kept him always
uprooting them, seeking his fortune, first in
the foothills near Berea at White's Station.
But he aimed ever toward the promised land,
the Bluegrass, where always the next farmstead,
the next town, the next crossroads store would make
of Thomas House a prosperous man, would make
his family healthy, happy. They grew to twelve.
Out by the roots Thomas pulled them, over
and over, just as they got to know the teacher
at whatever country schoolhouse, and got
longed-for invitations to the neighbors' dances.

At thirteen, Mary's hands were red
from scalding diapers, and she was deft,
but not so gentle, at tucking shirttails,
wiping noses of the little ones. Martha,
overwhelmed, grew weak and sickened,
while more and more Tom left bright Mary, good
at numbers and with customers, to keep
the store while he went fishing, set tobacco,
played nine-card rum, or tended to his hounds.
At White's Station, then at Poosey Ridge,
at Paint Lick, and finally at Athens, the family
half grown now, he thought he'd found
at last the land of milk and honey: white
clapboard cottage with pretty gingerbread;
the big high-ceilinged store with walnut shelves
and tin-topped counter; rich bottomland

to rent; and the relief and gratitude
of law-abiding citizens that this strange
mountain man would try to keep the peace
in Athens, a still unruly frontier town.
Elected magistrate, Tom was the only man
among the neighbors brave enough, or fool
enough, to want the job. He was policeman,
jury, judge, and jailer all in one.

And Mary kept the books, knew how much flour
to trade for pecks of wormy apples, rusty
pole beans, knew how to keep the men from
dipping in the cracker barrel, spitting
on the stove, loafing too long on the porch.
She collected all accounts, even Robert Martin's
and Maybelle Short's, hard cases Tom had given up.
She was courted by the bravest bachelors in the county,
the few not cowed by her straight eyes,
her honest tongue: the doctor from Virginia
and the prosperous keeper of the rival store.
But at thirty, her mother dead, her sisters grown
and caring for the little ones, she chose a poor man,
Pick, soon richer than the others all combined.
He labored in tobacco, in his cattle
for fourteen hours a day when light was long.
And this she liked—she was a worker, too.
He'd sworn he'd never marry till he owned
a farm himself, expected hands he hired
(both white and black) for fifty cents a day
to work as hard as he did for himself.

At forty, he had his farm at last, had found
this stern and queenly maid who suited him
exactly. Too peculiar to dismount and come
inside to court, he sat upon his horse
across the road whenever time allowed,
for three long years, in winter and in summer,
his favorite hound, Old Thunder, asleep
at Traveler's feet, and waited for some business
to bring his Mary out of doors. She paid
him little mind, preferred the custom of her
father's store to choosing from among these men.

Ever restless, Thomas, missing Martha,
still not rich, but disillusioned, threatened
by a man he'd jailed, moved his worn-out
family one step back into the mountains.
Then Pick would ride all day to pay his court
at Sander's Ferry deep in Garrard County.
In June of 1900, in Thomas's dark parlor,
they married with the youngest children peeking
through the banisters. "Do you take this woman
to be your lawful wedded wife?" "Certainly,
certainly," answered Pick in the Virginia tones
he never lost. Next day, she rode with him
back into Athens, starting another life.

At thirty-one she started having babies,
more boys than girls, all sturdy, keen,
and definite as briars. None died until old age.
Pick delighted in them, having gone so long

without them, spoiled them, doomed them,
with her help, vowed he'd go on earning
Bluegrass farms until he got them one apiece.
And there was violence in it: Pick's nephew
Crazy Jim (Pick raised him from a boy) came
one morning, brandishing a knife, to play
with Charlie B. Her scared heart flamed as Jim's
empty blue eyes filled her own. She handed him
her baby, praying she would get him back alive.
All morning, from inside the darkness
of the kitchen, she watched, scarcely breathing,
shushing the others, frightened, too, as the man
and baby played beside the icehouse with the kittens.
At dinnertime, Jim handed Charlie B. inside
to her and took his own plate to the shade.

The many years of loss (her brother, mother,
sister) made it hard for her to give her love
its head, even to her children, always
wanting of her. But if she was not tender,
still she always tended them, and all her tasks:
her garden, turkeys, guineas, chickens.
She sold eggs and cream in town on Thursdays,
planted hollyhocks and roses by the cabin,
tiger lilies down the driveway lined with poplars,
always keeping careful records of what
she planted when and where, when she set
the guineas and the geese, when they hatched,
how many hatchlings lived. Each night
she took her diary from the chifforobe

beside the hearth and wrote about the weather,
who'd come to visit, which sons stayed out
all night the night before, and in the back
she kept a list of neighbors' deaths that year.

Once at dinner on a July afternoon
heavy with storm, with sixteen at her table
(the children, Pick, the threshers, and herself)
the kitchen cat, stealing Teddy's drumstick,
bit through the palm of his small hand. She rose,
staunched the baby's punctures, and then flung
the cat against the chopping block,
and with the axe chocked off his head
onto the woodpile and resumed her place
at table. When Grace, third oldest, Pick's
favorite, crept behind her rocking chair one day
and, thinking it a good joke on her mother,
pulled her somersaulting over backwards
with the baby, Mary snatched the buggy whip
and raised a single welt on Grace's
back that neither of them ever could forget.

At forty-four she said to Pick, "No more"
(three girls, four boys, all pretty, full of vim,
calling in the night, pulling at her apron,
wanting another biscuit, piece of chicken,
or needing a button or a patch). She ordered,
from Sears Catalogue, twin rosewood beds.
Outside the Blue Room where they slept, she nailed
a trace chain from her father's plowing harness.

When night winds swung it up against the boards,
its music brought back mountain days to her,
the red-roofed house beside Rockcastle River
where in 1893 her removal had begun.

When Pick was in bed, dying, he thought all
the years had folded back into their flower,
that he was at Belle Brezing's famous house
in Lexington. "Oh, please, don't tell Mary,"
he pleaded, raveling at the feed-sack quilt.
"Tell her I'll be home directly."

Older, Mary refused to set her foot
in Athens. Each Saturday, Jim Buck put on
a gold-braided chauffeur's cap and drove her
to the Jim Nix Cafeteria in Lexington.
Looking neither left nor right, she passed
the Athens crossroads, passed the store she used
to keep; dressed in black finery and gold beads,
she rode the long Queen Mary, her own Buick,
bought with her savings from her cream and fowl.
Then she felt rich beyond her father's dreams.

On these bright Saturdays as she leaves home,
she sometimes feels herself a girl again,
beside her mother on the wagon seat,
holding tight to skinny Hiram as they left
the red-roofed house beside Rockcastle River.
And she remembers how she looked back
from the last bend in the rutty road

through tears galling as her mother's,
until the trees obscured the white-washed house,
the red roofs of the farm where they were born,
Martha's dowry sold to stake them in the Bluegrass.

Finally, she can't believe her life has gone,
that Pick is dead. She sees her children's lives
convolute with trouble. She tells whoever listens,
"If I had it to do over, I wouldn't have a single child."
Puzzlement clouds her eyes with cataracts.
Small strokes dull her tongue. Her house is empty as
October sky. Beside the hearth, her jaw slacks;
she watches embers die. Sometimes she hears
her children's voices crying for a touch
she cannot give. Inside her chifforobe,
the five-year diaries press her days in locked-
up pages. In her balls of string, her rows
of canning jars, her boxes of old lace
and linens, articles of life all stacked
on shelves, arranged in drawers, in pantries,
her mind shifts, settles like motes in thick,
last rays of sun. Her white hair, like a dandelion,
seems to froth as she nods in her chair.
Her thoughts soon drift away. Dark winds
will lift her memories, seed by weightless seed,
into cold currents. Like smoke, they rise,
disperse, are nothing in the darkening sky.

Above the parlor mantel now she still
is straight, her gaze sharp as the poker

on the hearth, a presence that her house, the yards,
the barns arranged themselves around; her husband
and the children in their orbits, too. Her hard
young jaw, fresh from the mountains, so definite
in this picture, now juts from my child's face
as it jutted from my father's. In that gold leaf
I see and know her more and more as I go
where she has gone. Above sad eyes, the chain
of her dark hair is wound into a crown.

Late Poems

I

Train Window

1965

That face of mine looks me straight in the eye.
The train, like a nagging mother, rails
and whines at me that I have lost my head,
and I could save my face,
but sit and watch it, fixed on a glass plate,
wiping across the reflecting back of night.

2010

In the subway window I see myself
among the others, not just me, my face
heavy with jowls, my eyes in shadow, not
as clever by half, no wit to spare. My head,
still looking back from its dark pane, has come
to understand decapitation. It is not illegal.

1965

But what could I do? It was snatched
before I knew what on earth was coming off.
Out there whole worlds pass by
and all my empty eyes can say
is they've seen me, and that is lean, lean news.

2010

In this tube of light burrowing like a mole
beneath New York, I and my fellows sit
shoulder to shoulder intimate in our heat.

In the black window I see beside me a boy,
rangy, gangsta, a wire trailing from his ear,
spasming to a beat I faintly hear over the chirp
of breaks, the rasp of metal wheels on the tracks.
Upon my other shoulder the head
of a leathery man bounces in sleep,
his hardhat precarious upon his knee.
They're familiar to me as husbands
as we tunnel through the dark.

1965

But I meant not to take this sitting down,
intend to crack this case; mean once again
to look something besides me square in the eye.
I'll ride out the night, no matter if it's long
as all black space behind the stars and moon,
for when it pales, so must that glassy face.
Perhaps it will not be because
my chair is empty as the cold gray bowl of dawn.

2010

At my stop I leave the picture,
the black window, and climb into
the light day. As I wait to cross
the street, a grocer from the corner stand
sweeps toward the storm sewer
a spill of grape tomatoes: so scarlet
on the wet, black pavement
among the rush of legs and feet!
On the glassy street

the falling sun silvers the city,
flashes in angles, brutal as Armageddon,
shining like the rapture. I walk into
into this blinding light while in the dark below
my chair's not empty. Somebody
warms between the boy, the man.

In October

The maple's green
hung on until last night's
hard frost
torched its used-up leaves.
And now the sunset light
inflames the tree
with fever you can see,
that eats it in a flash
of slow, falling fire.

Haiku for the New Year, 2010

How short a season
do we wear this dress of flesh.
How soon it tatters, sags!

Winter Moon

When I open my curtains at daybreak
the fey old moon sits on a branch
ready to flap away into the half-light
above the luminous triangles
of houses in the next street.
Rising, shrinking, the bright bone
is buried then revealed again
in the slow smudge of clouds.

A Poem

A poem is a bird that flies on many wings,
brings us to life in stories not our own.
A poem makes a voice inside our heads that sings
of the tender, inch-tall oak
that cracks apart the acorn hard as stone.

November Wind

Boanerges neighs and bucks.
Through nights, through days
he gallops on. Before him
trees bend like grass.
On his back, winter rides in.

Iddy Romps

Through skeins of sleep I hear my cat
drop her acorn on the hardwood,
roll it down the stairs. In the dark
she gallops on bare boards, and I hear
her squeeze-toy whistling. At daybreak
I come almost awake
and make her body out, still at last
beside my bed, fallen like a blot
on the Rorschach of the oriental rug.

She watches me. I see
the black holes of her eyes,
rich and deep as a mine
in the dawning, sideways light.
Her shadow grows
a twin among the rug's phantasms.
While the new day gathers,
her eyes fix
my wooly, lumpish body,
as if it were a dance,
some quick shuttling
of warf and woof that she sees
weaving together again
unlikely, predictable Jane.

Crows

As metaphor for thought and mind
I thought of crows in winter trees,
riding ragged branches through the wind,
as raucous before roost as words.

By threes, by two, then one by one
they leave my vacant mind to comb
with hungry teeth the tangled skies
and circle home, past sight, beyond the rise.

Empty tree, whipped by the wind,
old head, stand metaphor for mind.

Out of Season

On a dark day
in February
from a field away
came a bird's trill
(a warbler maybe,
passing through,
or a wren
who'll sing
by the backdoor when
the season turns)
pronouncing the sufficient word
of sun, leaves, blooms
and the sky's blue rooms,
so contrary
to this bone cold,
dark day
in February.

What Does it Take to Be Happy

Has something tragic happened to you?
or yours? No matter—you can still be happy.
Are you right with yourself? No?
We're all divided against ourselves
in ways too numerous to mention.

But animal comfort helps,
and a modicum of competence,
plus the well-being of those you love.

Definitely, the bright vinegar of winter sun
pouring around you as you lie recovering
from flu, and ears to hear the sparrows'
silly cheeping, praising the false spring.

Sudden Storm on Eleuthera

O strangeness of the sea and sky
when thunder cracked out of the blue,
and glistenings of the plain horsefly
made dark rainbows as it flew.

My Ease

When we were young, death
astonished us: loved faces
went gray or yellow, and bodies
of grandfather, uncles, aunts
disappeared under the bedclothes
never to be seen again;
or a gentle, sad-eyed spaniel
splintered the small bones
of a gosling,
sharp beneath its down.

Now, death is a habit,
having taken, one by one,
the creatures of that first world.
The undertaker, the son of the son
of the first I knew, greets me as
a faithful customer. And I, though I
relish still the thrumming of my body,
the wheel of seasons, the laughter
and talk of my children and their
children, I don't dread darkness,
or lying down on the earth
and taking my ease.

Bird and Bear

I looked through my black window into black
and saw the great bear on his endless track
that leads him round the pole, back to his start.
Until the hatching sun shall break his heart

he paces in his circle through our sleep,
restless for his own that's long and deep,
stays till the sky becomes a cave of light,
retreats into his blazing, brilliant night.

Now comes the golden bird that flies its way
as if a thousand years were but a day,
whose eye sheds light in watching busy men
and, molting, drops to feed its fire again

in the tall tree of its death and birth
that stands in Egypt underneath the earth,
it finds the silence of the song it sings
and into ashes folds its glistening wings.

Then from the winter of cold, hungry rest
the bear will rise as from a flaming nest
to transfix with a bright but lightless eye
the dreaming men who sleep beneath the sky;

not as the bird in seeing to create
but, watching through the dark half of their fate,

to see that sleeping eyes shall always find
the black beast at the bottom of the mind.

The bird can keep the dream that is the day,
but when its time is run, it cannot stay.
Behind the daylight sky I see in black
the bear careening slowly on his track.

Hurray

For a moment today, I,
an old woman, lying
bundled in a hammock,
looking up into a tree,
with a child's eye see
the fact of sunshine
on gray bark, high
up against a vague
November sky
empty, as the branch is
of leaves and sense:
the sky, the branch,
the shining world itself,
not metaphor
for something else.

September

Rain falls on the roof,
on wilting leaves. In worn fields
a new peace settles.

March Wind

pushes past the corner of the house,
its low voice saying its own
slow, muddle-headed thoughts,
keeping up its mulling worry.

by morning, its stupid graffiti smears
the windows. Katzenjammer
hieroglyphics slither downwards
when I touch the pane.

Letters for Butterfly

1

Butterfly,
I am an old cello.
You a piccolo on the way to
clarinet.
What music will you
play with colored wings,
the dust that gathers
light?

There is, of course, no flight
to speak of.
But please, listen to the beat
of this stillness

waiting.

2

Your fire, butterfly,
is ire made red
by all those things
you chose to cling to
and could not.
But tell me: is this net I cast
the crown you dreamed about
that night you cried alone

forsaken by all flowers,
or else
the darkest pond that you so fear?

I am, as you well know,
only water.
I am cloud
when we touch.

3

Oh, butterfly!
Long ago there once lighted
an evil moth upon my face.
She settled there for weeks
and made me hers.
She chained both of my legs
and stuffed all my ten fingers.
The doctors thought I'd die.
And so did I.

She left one day
as strangely as she came.
But doctors say that moths
like that
can dwell inside you long,
like wolves who wait upon their prey.

Two butterflies live now
inside my heart:

an old one who claims that I belong to her,
a young one who doesn't know she's there.

4

Can you spell, butterfly?
Yes, *smell* I know you can.
For in the garden where I sweat
you sometimes light upon my skin
to feast on pheromones.
But when I see you flutter so
among lavenders and hydrangeas,
I want to think that with your wings
you script to me some careless code.

And so,
you want to say *connect* but say *correct,*
you wish to write *behave* and do *behalf,*
you think you want to *throw* but you are *through,*
you put me down for *poem* when it's: *come.*

For this, the reading that I read,
the spell you cast, frail friend,
in that orthography of souls,
suffices.

I have no need of letters.
Your wings say all to me.

5

I learned tonight, dear butterfly,

that sex among you
"near the apex of the upper wings,
is a matter of a short and traverse stripe."
In some of you it's orange;
in others, it is white,
"though distinctions are so slight
it is often overlooked."

I wish to join that kingdom
of confusion!
So long as you distinct me
and I you
along our merry flight,
I care not what my color is:
be it orange, be it white.

6

You dare, butterfly.
You dare go there
for air.
Not here, not near.
There, far, away, yonder.
I see, I wonder

would you
see me, or ponder,
away, from far,
fly back to me
to dare to be
air,

near,
here.

7

One fine day,
when the robins nest again,
we'll notice
in the far horizon,
nearing on the sea,
a tiny pair of wings.
I, then, without replying,
will hide awhile,
in silence,
to keep from dying
from joy.

All I say
will come true, butterfly.

Te lo prometto.

8

Butterfly, you tell me,
with a flutter of wings,
that I know what you know
and that you love I know it.
Yet flutter more, I beg of you,
to know this:
that the day you see me

knowing you
I'll love the knowledge
of loving you

even more.

9

I am your water
you are my light
thought I caught
butterflies whispering,
riding together, hardly astir,
apexes rubbing,
gravity-fighting
until,
energy spent,
sweat and dust dangling,
one huge crash-landing,
all of a piece,
lawned.

Water light
echo stirred
fading
as sprinkles punctual
boomed.

10

Your arrow strikes,

butterfly,
where it hurts most.
Cupid's bows,
Diana's lances,
Pocahontas' smile
could not have entered
where yours dislodge away
this sense of self.
Those Sagittarian mirrors
have seared with lasers,
the gentle burden of your eyes,
the golden apple of my age,
the clock's serenity.

I fear that I may not
be brave to fight you.
The fire of this love
will have its say.

11

Sex with you, butterfly.
Sex would be, well,
difficult.
Still, possible I think.
And, of course, beautiful.
But, how? Where?
In what position?
While lighting, or in flight?
Perhaps as . . . caterpillars?

Yes, or chrysalis,
better yet!
Oh for the comfort
of cocoons!
Upon some petals,
as we suck all
that pollen.
At night. At dinnertime,
away from moths
that wish to eat our love,
and bite each other?

Embrace me, butterfly,
with both wings.
And I shall drink your nectar
in the Spring.

12

Tonight I realize, butterfly,
it actually won't matter
how many of these letters
I end up writing to you.
The heart's content,
the body's pain,
my laptop's entertainment,
all shall be in vain
to make you come to me
to join in ecstasy.
The dreams of an old man

who dreamed of being young,
or living once again,
are nightmares that will not
be lived by either one of us,
or both at once.

The epitaphs I write
tonight as I succumb
to papers that are filled
by prodigies of light
will not be read by you.
I dream this once again.
I dream of you
too late.

13

Absence makes the heart
grow *fondo.*
Hondo, as in deep,
butterfly.
There seems to be no bottom
in this freefall of a dream.
The depths of love grow greater
as absence flows
from deep inside this stream.
Your long-stemmed fingers,
your stature high above,
the way you stare at emptiness
are things that never happened,

or else some ghosts that roar?

Absence, butterfly,
drills greater holes
than one can scarce imagine.
I know her name and know her.
Her depths are all I have.

14

Should nothing ever happen,
butterfly,
there's always flight, I know.
I know because in this
profound admixture of happiness and sad,
facing the loss of coffee times
yet certain of times of faith,
the sweetest pain
invades my chest so hard
that I enjoy it.
At times like these
I float away and there,
among the nightingales,
a Painted Lady rises
with spots so blue
I sense that they
inspect me.

There is no loss in flight
with one embracing two.

I fly with her, my love,
as if I were with you.

15

John was wrong, butterfly.
Beauty is not truth,
nor truth beauty.
He was thinking of an urn,
perhaps an ancient Grecian one,
where maidens run about
without worry of
persecution.
Beauty in butterflies, I've found,
is a matter of distrust
of all those lepidopterists,
intent on dessication
to preserve.
So closely do they try
to study beauty,
that beauties flee their love.
Their truth, then,
yours that is,
is that all that declaration
goes for naught.
For in their winsome flight
those Painted Ladies search
for ugly skippers
whose blindness, or their smarts,
arrests their ever telling them
the truth.

But John was also right, butterfly.
The truth of beauty and your own:
that is all I knew on earth,
that is all I need to know.

16

Never tell a butterfly
you love her.
She'll rebuke you,
she'll find you mad,
she'll think you're lying,
or out to get her.
For butterflies believe
the beauty that they have,
their burning magnet,
attracts those moths
for all wrong reasons.
They seek the body,
not the flight.
They want the eyespots,
not the wings.
They wish to bind that insect
to their might.

Observe, oh butterfly:
a butterfly
never flies like a bird.
That beauty seems a burden,
a burden quite absurd.

17

I wonder sometimes, butterfly,
if I'm a woman, too.
For one,
I talk to butterflies.
At other times, all day,
I glow at how
they dress themselves
and chat from gardens
to what's next.
And then, to share the gossip
of flowers in their stead,
or dreaming how you travel
from kitchen to your bed.
But worst of all is crying.
I cry like them, like you,
when something hits my heart,
or feel that I must go.
The mourning that I know,
the ghosts of lovers past.

I wonder who I am,
oh butterfly of mine.
Tonight, as I remember,
I wonder if I'm you.

18

The freer you are,
the better you'll be.

The better you'll be
the greater you are.
The greater you are,
the miner you'll be.
The miner you'll be,
the freer you are,

butterfly.

19

Before leaving Butterfly drew me
a nice picture on my skin.
A tiny one gathering together
a river, a boat, a boatman,
a small portion of her light,
colors whose deft distribution
only she knows.
Her eyes have it, you see,
and I say,
for the manner that she looks
at walls, at me,
or that river
does constitute a landscape
all its own.

Tu mirada es un paisaje.
Tus ojos, el sol de Dios.

Then I rushed to look at pictures
very deep inside my eyes

and sang all night that old mantra
that returns her to my door:

You are my picture, my darling.
I am frame,
an empty wall.

20

A forest, I'll have you know,
can scare a butterfly
away.
Big, dark, deep.
Above all, old,
with trees with barks as coarse
as welts and scars
from fights, and beasts
and wars.
She lightly steps in for flowers
yet fears that the trees will fall,
animals that prey upon animals,
the cries all night of ghosts
that live on sunlight,
like people.

Butterfly fears are real.
I see them daily, from lairs,
withdraw despite my calling
for help.
For in my dreams

I wish I were a butterfly in Winter,
not just a forest
pretending that it's Spring.

21

She just hung there
like a statue made of gems.
Those emerald legs,
green tears reminding me of me,
a sparkling torso
and eyes like hers, of sky
in winters that are pure,
hung there
below golden horns
and golden rope
as if chained all there to take,
hanging cozy
in a box.

Yet I know that some day
I must give away
that butterfly to Butterfly,
believing that that day,
the day she comes to get me,
I may well be hers
all wrapped,
like a gift.

Night Snow

A simple fall,
a shawl of snow,
will wrap up all
the land in white,

will fall across
the wounded earth
erasing signs of loss,
all notices of blight.

When we awake
to this new world
old Eden's days
return unfurled

in morning light.

Haiku

Unlovely locusts,
broken by wind and lightning,
swagged now in silken blooms.

I've seen no fresher
sight than new leaves against blue
newly washed spring sky

Honeysuckle

All the July day
the moth, shy of sun
and the black sky behind
it, sleeps upside
down among the vines.
Lulled by the bees'
basso and the perfume
that lures them, she
droops like a pistil from
a flower's ivory neck.

When nightfall rouses
her, she flusters
from her powdery
rest to seek out darkness.
But she can't get
past the back porch
bulb, can't ride her frantic
wings into the darkest
darkness where she yearns
to go.

The Cattle Man

He walked among his cattle like God
in his new creation speaking
to them matter-of-factly as one might
speak to a bright but daydreaming child.
Sometimes he sang odd vowels to them.

The cattle nudged each other, butting,
pushing round the trough while he
secured the block of Moorman's salt,
rough on their caressing tongues,
delicious as if it were a calf.

From the hair of their rippling hides
rose rankness of cud, manure, fresh-
ripped grass, live leather. The tassels
of their tails flicked the green flies
grazing on their flanks.

Their hooves excited the baked
ground, pocked from their shoving
to the trough in winter mud.
How they flung round
their rubbery necks at gadflies!

He walked among his cattle at ease
on earth: the bright convex
summer in their eyes liquid as tears,
jeweled orbs regarding him
that day in onyx and in amber.

II

Diana of Times Square

The simple sun can shine Kentucky bright,
but subtly and more richly shines Diane
the moon, the woman whose complexities of light
weave richer goods than her near-blinding twin

Apollo, simply there or not, but she
sheds light in phases, in dark or at the full,
she's constant to the earth she spreads with green
while currents, tides, and time all feel her pull.

So at the crossroads of the world, Diane,
luminous and blunt, hunts across the silver sky
until good morning breaks across the land:
she fades but lights our television's eye.

Fall of the Year

Penniless women, their children, and ragtag
woodsmen came to Kentucky, refugees
from the stench of settlements in Virginia
and North Carolina, to claim a share of
the Iroquois meadow lands, into a forest
so shadowed that the sun lit only
its canopy, a golden roof above their heads
vulnerable as a baby's crown.

Numberless as fish, fat squirrels swam
in zigzags across the Ohio, the Licking,
the Kentucky. Buffalo ran the traces,
thousands in a herd, turning aside
only for full grown trees that stood
between them and a good salt lick.

Time doesn't move, so they are still
here: the animals, the virgin trees
the women cooking over fire or bathing
a child for burial when thaw comes,
the men scouting for meat or salt.
In this waste of paradise
A log house, now forgotten under

vinyl siding, lit by golden arches,
glows behind McDonald's, full still
of rememberers of the chance
that dropped us here where churches

metal-skinned like warehouses resound
with praises staged, amplified,
produced like television shows.

At day's end, waves of grackles
sail like runes into the wintry sky,
an undertow of birds riding the year's
outgoing tide, their voices, strange
as those in our own mouths,
repeat the story of which the name
cannot be named.

The Duties of the Old

People talk to you a great deal about your education, but some good, sacred memory, preserved from childhood, is perhaps the best education. [If one] carries many such memories with him into life, he is safe to the end of his days, and if one has only one good memory left in one's heart, even that may sometime be the means
of saving us.

Dostoevsky, *The Brothers Karamozov*

To tell the young about the country you've crossed into
To grow more patient
To recall your body's prime with a savor near to appetite
To dream at night and bring bright visions back
To hiss at dogs, bark at cats, make trouble as you go
To let slights slide from your heart like daily tasks out of your head
To read your stacked up books before the letters fade
To summon to your inner eye the faces of your childhood
To spend your days like coins warmed inside your pocket
To honor trees, always growing, up and down
To hear ancestors' voices when they speak
To drink your time in draughts
To call things by their real names (we die; we do not pass)
To tell your stories, not too often or too long
To serve memory like a side dish at your feast of days
To turn easily to sleep again in the empty watches of the night
To eat the roughest bread and drink clear water
To take the light of each new morning into your startled eyes
To leave your windows open to each season's music
To keep your rooms alive with rituals
To wear, like a queen's train, the cape of your long past

To wear your body's scars like medals
To work until work's pleasure drains away
To hold your bones upright
To set less stock in flesh, like fruit, that's overripe

For Audrey on the Occasion of Her 75th Birthday

My Made Bed

I am walking down the sunny street
when a picture of my made bed
springs to mind, bringing comfort
out of no particular discomfort, order
out of minimal disorder, and the sense
of sanctuary on a peaceful morning.

I had smoothed my body's warmth
from the sheet, plumped my head-shape
from the pillow, and wiped the covers
clean of wrinkles.

Now I cross into the snarls of traffic
passing strangers whose minds
churn with images unknowable
to me. At home my bed lies ready
to receive me, to ferry me across
the deep unfathomed waters
of the coming night.

Eve in the Orchard

The woman stands in shadow thick as night,
an apple in her hand, apples
brimming from her baskets,
trees disappearing into vapors of light.

Although she comes to gather apples,
a tingle in her breast rises
at the touch of the sweet air.
"Would Adam like to taste?" she wonders.

"No," he says, "it's all yours. I've eaten."
A crow squawks from a treetop. Another
razzes back. The apple's thick skin warms
in her grip. The dew is cold around her feet.

She stands in shadow; her head swims
in light. The trees grow mean
and dwarfish in the distance.
The apple, when she bites it, smells like him.

Holding onto the basket, her back straight,
she spits the bitter stem, the black seeds
from her mouth red as the apple.
On the morning of that first day, the first fall,

she waits in all of Eden's brutal glory
for another reading of her story.

Indiana Shoot-out

In shirts of many colors, emblazoned
with strange words (Depauw, Augustana,
Greencastle, Vevey), girls of all shapes
crowd toward the field-house shouting loud
halloos and vaunts to familiar rivals. Their
fathers pull coolers on wheels, their mothers
trundle rolls of quilts and comforters, picnic
baskets, little sisters. Four courts, four games
at once, the thumping of four balls, five
times a day: the shoot-out.

The tall ones (zero body-fat), the stocky ones
(muscular as boys) flap their defensive wings
fierce with disinterest, their legs like Slinkies.
Their coach bends over as if punched
in the gut, then laughs, exhorts "Defense,
defense!" smacks his sweat-slick head when
the girl who stole from him dribbles through
traffic into the paint, leaps, and, with lethal
motion toward the hole, fires the ball:
impervious and silly as a frantic heart.

At Cumae

This room is too small.
Pieced from the upstairs hall
It cuts off the light, walls in
The only window to the maple tree,
Thick-trunked now, but still a sapling
When my house was built. This bathroom,
barely big enough to turn around in, with its
half-sized tub where I lie curled, amniotic, my spine
a tendril like the maple used to be, allowing gravity
to let my body go, becomes kaleidoscopic. In the green
light of morning, I'm like the Sibyl in her bottle, younger
in her heart and mind than in the body she forgot. I
Wish for timely death. But for now there's water
enough to buoy me. Its tongues lick and warm
my knotted muscles as I drift and turn on
the wheel of sunlight falling to this
glass through leafy rooms. Raptures
twitch the leaves upon their stems.
Numberless they dance with their
Own shadows, winking, whirling,
feinting flowers of light that
tumble on the walls of this
small room where in a bliss
of water I suspend my life.

My Tin Ear

Faint now the song of the furnace
I barely hear the clap of my neighbor's
screen door. Just the tag end
of my friend's compliment as I walk
away. Distant the door chime
when my good ear lies
on my pillow. The rumble
and horn of the two a.m. train
only brushes the skin of my sleep.
All but inaudible
the headlong chorus of robins
in the May dawn. So begins
a great silence.

From My Passing Car I See in the Cemetery

black winter trees against the snow.
Row after row of stones, each topping a mound
pillowy as a new-made bed.
Under two of these, side by side lies
what remains of my mother and father,
not spooned as they slept
when I fled to their bed from a childish
dream, but stiff, formal as relief
upon sarcophagi, so cold they lost
touch as surely as Odysseus and his mother
in the Underworld, when he reached out
to hold her and she dissolved like smoke.
My parents also their flesh, the hair
on their arms (hers bright, his dark);
their cheeks (hers silk, his like sand),
collapsed; the bowls of their skulls
empty now; the fountains of their breaths
stopped; their sturdy bones deconstructing
molecule by molecule, down in the dark
under this blanket of snow, clasped
in the black arms of the black trees.

He's Off to the MLA

A fire burns in this picture,

eats her formless witch's dress,
her stomping high-tops,
her furious flaming face,
her used up, hanging breast,
her many fingered scarlet hands
flung out in dismissal and good-bye.

The children peer from the pockets
of the maelstrom, their wondering prayerful eyes
unafraid. One, diapered, flies out
on the scalding wind, clinging for his life,
like her ideas, her visions.
Hot and full as sausages,
the dogs (Hambone, Possum, Bingo),
their tails hooking at her hems, grovel
toothsome, at his feet.

Except him, one and all race across the burning
plain, toward the fiery window of their house.
Only he, dandy in his bowtie, his gray closed face,
definite as a stone in his dark overcoat,
hatches visions and revisions, under his fedora.
We know he feels the heat of her
strong heart, with his.
In this picture even the shut eyes see.
This is not a picture without love.

My First Friends

Under the porch
a checkerboard of sunlight
on the brown silk dirt.
Footsteps on the boards above.
I am small, quiet.
"Jane, your lunch is ready. Ja-ane."
I crawl out into the hot light.

My place. A place
where Maggie and Jaggie live
in a spell of darkness. All night
they sweep their rugs
flecked with moonlight.
Don't move away while
I am gone. Keep house
here till I come back.
Tomorrow, I'll help you
    move into the hollow locust.

Landing in Atlanta

Two by two, as orderly as the ark, as close
as spouses breathing together through the night,
we sit obedient and passive, powering down
our electronic devices, in preparation for
landing, "An excellent view of the city
on the right below, the mountain on the left."

The pilot maneuvers us to ground,
descending step by step through mesas
of cloud and air, and with the thump
of landing gear he springs the snare, then
guides us smack onto the tarmac, the
solid earth that translates us from watery
blue where, serene, we sailed above
the flood of all our earthly parables.

Abraham Lincoln in Kentucky

"I was born, and have ever remained, in the most humble walks of life.
. . . I happen, temporarily, to occupy the White House. I am a living wit-
ness that any of your children may come here, as my father's child has."

—Abraham Lincoln

Two hundred years ago, near the gash of earth called
Sinking Spring, Abraham Lincoln first saw light.
Far from the reach of sunshine, dark water filters
from the rock in that deep limestone cave
whose black hollows reappeared in his country
face that some called ugly, gave it the shadow
of sorrow, but also the steady gentleness
and kindliness that radiates from absence
of vengefulness, of selfish vision, of partisanship,
of easy blindness to the wrong within
the right and the right within the wrong.
In North and South, in peace and war, in slave
and free he saw children, women, men all
human and all suffering. His vision cleared to this,
despite his own hard griefs. He broke free of all
that bound him from his unschooled childhood,
from the work-crushed world of his father Thomas,
his grandfather Abraham, killed by Indians set
to repel white settlers from their hunting ground.

Born to this struggle, Lincoln still became a saint,
if you understand a saint to be a flawed, too human,
being, a rare one who finds devotion to good

greater than his own, one who never loses sight
of himself, a man, only, among many men. In youth,
gangly, strong, his pants always too short, he loved
to win: childish games, and, later, wrestling matches,
and, later still, cases at the law, attention from the women.
But, sorrowing for his mother Nancy, taken by milk
fever when he was nine years old, and for his sister
Sarah dead in childbirth nine years later,
he learned books as if his life depended on it
(as it did). Failing at store-keeping and at love,
but always starting over, he grew toward balance,
calm. The only grudge he harbored was toward
his sister's in-laws, who, saving money,
sought help too late and let her die. The son
of a sad mother, Abe was often sad, but his sadness
opened his heart to others and the world, did not
close him off in bitterness.

Thomas, not understanding Abe's bookish ways
despaired of him, thought him lazy, pushed
his needy boy away. But in choosing Sarah Bush
for wife, Thomas chose the mother his son needed.
Abe grew up hurt but loved, good-natured, merry,
game, as well as sad. He could charm the bark
right off a hickory and tell a story like Scheherazade.

Without a model for the destiny he wished for, he
undertook the hazards of the usual human life,
(marriage, children, calling) though skittish of it all
and troubled in his choices.

After the sweetness of the doomed Anne Rutledge
and his paper dalliance with Mary Owens, he came
to wed the well-bred, sharp Miss Mary Todd,
almost his equal in political acumen, always believing
in his greatness. With the births of their four sons
(three to die untimely),she to him was always
"Mother," and, after the fashion of the day, he
to her was ever "Mr. Lincoln." With his boys
he loved to eat ice cream, to egg them on in mischief,
which caused scandal on the train that carried them
to Lexington for his first visit with the Todds.
At the Old Soldiers Home, one summer afternoon
to his boys' delight, he and Edwin Stanton climbed
a tree to rescue peafowl from the tangled vines.
But shadows fell upon his face when Eddie died
at three, and Willie, who charmed all Washington,
at twelve. A father so unlike his own, yet he
survived these deaths and heard his calling.
The war he ordered, setting kinsmen against
kinsmen, scalded off his rhetoric, clarified
his words, stripped away his posturing, clear-cut
a channel from his heart into his head, leaving
his truths untainted by his words.

Alexander Gardner's November 8, 1863 Photograph of Lincoln

His picture in an oval frame hung above our sofa
in my childhood. I saw the sadness in his face,
knew that he knew sorrow, his left eye always
seeing something darker than the right.

Gardner's lens saw him as he was days before
he went to Gettysburg. Shadows everywhere
except his lighted brow; the left face older
than the right, the perfect bow of his upper lip
set straight across the fullness of the lower,
the furrows from his nose down to his mouth,
above the shock of dark beard touched with white.
His headstrong hair barely tames into a part.
His eyebrows hood unsparing eyes denying
nothing that they see; his loose, left eye,
willed to baleful focus with the right, sees what
the other doesn't quite. His bow tie sits askew;
his left ear swells bigger than the right. No
symmetry, but something rarer and more beautiful.

He struggled long to claim his better self:
open friend, conscientious enemy,
smitten father, patient husband of a silly wife,
political tactician, teller of stories, speaker
from a clear heart, wily commander in chief,
all this in the puzzle of his human face.

But an unfamiliar light beacons there,
shines from his brow above the darkness of his eyes.
Sanity: as odd, where people are, as the pileated bird.
But, oh, it freed a people and kept a nation whole.

At Peterson's Boarding House

APRIL 14–15, 1865

This dust was once the man,
Gentle, plain, just and resolute, under whose cautious hand,
Against the foulest crime in history known in any land or age,
Was saved the Union of these States.

—Walt Whitman

In the swampy streets of Washington in April,
far from the forests, farms, and springs of his
beginnings in Kentucky, Abraham Lincoln,
relieved at the slowing grind of war, decided
against another gruesome visit to Union
troops in the fallen capital, Richmond,
and, instead, without his bodyguard (already
in Virginia), he indulged his fancy for a play,
"Our American Cousin," a fluff that he had seen
before, that Mary begged him not to see again.
With her at Ford's Theater, he sank
gladly into darkness in the presidential box,
the story on the stage bright in his eyes,
when John Booth, a bad actor, joined him
in the shadows, slipping through unguarded
doors. Mary heard a scream, her own voice
gone ahead of what she could take in.
She flung herself, a shield, upon his ruptured
body. Chaos rose as the audience understood
what story was enacted. The posse
of men that hovers always near the powerful,

pushed her aside, gathered his sprawling limbs
as best they could, and shoving through
the panic of the mob, carried him and
his torn head across the muddy street and
up the steps of William Petersen's house.

Knowing then the gravity of his murder
to themselves who loved him, but also to the North,
the South, to history, they laid him
on the only downstairs bed, a Jenny Lind
so small they spread his six foot four deadweight
crossways on it. So small the room, a porch

once, low ceiling slanted outward, the men
all crowded round, his cabinet, advisors,
with scant space for Mary who left off
sobbing in the parlor long enough
to rush back to clutch his hand, touch,
unbelieving, his already marbling face.

Toward dawn, his noisy breaths came slowly
and finally not at all. All night the men had stood
shoulder to shoulder in their evening clothes,
or in their everydays from home, forgetful
of themselves, thinking only of his body, of
what was now to come, tears upon their faces
as for a father or a child.

After he let go his final breath, the room raw
with wordless anguish, Stanton, once his enemy,

spoke for all "Now he belongs to the ages,"
or, some heard him say, "the angels."

"Help, angels, make assay" to lift his spirit
off his awkward body, the light of sanity
gone out again, while in Kentucky far away
good water seeps through limestone rock
in the dark cave of the Sinking Spring.

Memorial Day 2010

A year of round numbers. All my life,
impossibly far off. Cheerful flags wave
from porches and poles. We have sacrificed
tender boys to the dark myth of war.

This afternoon, the heavy day cleared,
brightened to a brilliant heaven. Pillars
of white clouds rise like tombstones
or soldiers parading. Out of the blue
my dead mother and father draw
close. They abide in my body,
alive with a child's attention
to the world: the wardrobe where her silky
dresses hung, where I crawled to hear the far off
bell of silence; the granary where his grubbing
hoes, his levels, his rakes and scoop shovels
hung in the slant of afternoon sunlight
where I saw dust rise and fall
in the rays, like years that abruptly drifted
and leave us in each other's company,

while those clouds on Memorial Day
stack themselves up to the height of all
mortal things, each cloud moving itself
from within like a snake, one body
of motion, like a battalion marched off
by the generals, like a flight of birds veering,
wheeling, of one mind, mixing, building

like a cloud, tumbling, dissolving in the vistas
of the sky, in the golden failing light. In the golden failure of light
So am I. So are you.   in the failure of golden light

Night Beasts in the Backyard

Often as I fall asleep an owl mutters
in the yellowwood. As daydreams fade,
the owl stays, a horned blank
against a starless sky, riding on the wind
that zithers through the pines. Sunk
into himself, all head and gut, his eyes
searchlight across the paths of mice he's come
to murder. His cries muddle with the wind from
northern places, and lull me back to nothing,
my old home.

Last night in my driveway, I caught
in my high beam a coon, adopted daughter
of the town, plump as the fatted calf
on neighbors' garbage, her back arched high
as a cat's. She stared a slattern stare
from behind her bandit's mask, her bony
digits fingering the gravel. Then she loped
away, veering sideways, daring me
to outrage at her trespass
and her pillage.

One night last week, a possum scuttled
through the porch light. His feet moved him
but not the parts of his scrounging, slapdash,
patchwork self: head of sloth, hair of hog,
eyes unblinking as a snake's, his tail
pink as a tongue of cunning muscle—

he came here from beyond the pyramids,
descends from dinosaurs, from the dark
behind my yellow windows, brittle, clear
against the night.

All we beasts, familiar to each other as bodies
of our own, as plain as being; and strange
as if from outer planets of the dimmest galaxies,
cosmic, ancient, aboriginal as debris from broken
stars: all of us, what we were, what we are.

Now

I am seventy-one and I remember
my mother, after her long marriage,
alone in her house ten miles
from town. Now I live in the stillness
that surrounded her. I hear the echoes
that played in her ears. I am
familiar now with the price
she paid for the smile on her face
as she waved goodbye to all
of us after our Sunday visit.

Outside Eden

Your grown child's trouble isn't yours.
Her weeping isn't yours,
nor the fault-finding husband,
nor the cruel diagnosis.
Because these troubles are not yours,
you can, though your step is heavy,
open your garden gate each day,
set out to work, and then
at night lay out your supper, eat
with hunger, pay your bills, and
then put down your head and sleep,
though dreams may trouble you.
In the morning, you may even sit
a half-hour in the swing beneath
the shade tree, breathing in
the summer air, thankful
that what troubles come
your way, you suffer and
withstand.

       But your child's trouble
is the token of your promise
broken, nothing you have spoken, but
implicit in all your acts of mothering:
the heating of small jars of food,
the hat against the sun, the reaching
hand gripped beside the snarl of traffic.

Perhaps I thought I might be
the first to foil betrayal, resist
the fruit of that foul, lovely tree.

Mary Daniel

(After an Oil Portrait by Earl F. Fiske—1920)

At ease after a day's work at a white woman's house, she
doesn't know yet that this will be the measure
of her life. She believes that her slender body, the flower
of her mouth, the dark mirrors of her eyes, her silky limbs
will carry her far: her one big button, hopeful
as a silver dollar on her blue-striped dress, the white
ruffle of her jabot, starched against her skin.
She believes the promises of honeysuckle wafting
through the open window, though the chair spindle
cuts her back, the rough green table burns beneath
her arm, while the white curtains she ironed today
frame her. Outside, katydids chorus shrill monotonies
in their house of leaves. Even Earl makes her do
what she doesn't want: sit here in this picture.

III

May Weather

Because I knew you
the air shines blue as the backs
of the selfish jays bivouacking tree
to tree, high up among fresh leaves
that lean out on tender necks toward
a world where colors bright as kites
against this sky pluck back its edges
sharp as the black arrows
of the jays' territorial cries.

The Berry Bowls

Spring was your last season. Now it's here
again with its clatter of birds, with its promises
moving on the air, while the world closes
like water over the roofs of the deserted village
of your life. Last May I watched you shed
our necessary illusions of safety and sure
time, just as, after hard frost,
a tree lets go its leaves.

Earlier, in our fog of loss, we stopped
at a yard sale. For my sake
you feigned interest in six berry bowls
I bought, their gilded fruit ghost-like
from long use. By then you'd seen
your name on all the shards of ostracism—
you faced already toward the border
of another country. You knew you would not
sit in this spring's sun eating breakfast
from these bowls, their dimming gold.

Tantalus

In my favorite picture of you, you stand
in a leafy garden in Rome, Georgia,
your sixty-year-old torso twisted
like the Apollo Belvedere, but you
rest one hand on a dry-laid wall and
the other on your hip. You wear a starched
shirt and a yellow tie. You're here
on business. You look straight
at me behind the camera, your face
alive with a smile not yet broken
open. Sun lights your face and your hand
on the stone, while a single pen
warms in your breast pocket.
Above your head, a loaded
branch dangles a firmament
of cherries, mostly ripe, promising
this summer and others sure to come.
Neither of us thinks (I, framing you
in rocks, red fruit, and foliage; you,
looking backward through the camera, focusing
on me a happiness I cannot now imagine)
that even as we dallied in that garden,
a seed, stoic as a cherry stone, was rooting
in you: would snake its branches
to your brain, its taproot to your gut.

After Sundown

I wake abruptly in the dark
(no start that I remember)
when the street is silent,
and my mind a fat black
spider spinning out her endless
list of worries, jobs to do,
old hurts.

Once, to find my rest again,
I simply rearranged my body
close to yours, withdrew
into the halo of your warmth
like a turtle to its shell.
There, sorrow comforted,
sleep swiftly came.

Tonight at three a.m., the streets
deserted, my peace broken,
my bed cold, I find
the only rest I can:
I give up, turn on the light
and seek the poor word
for this poem.

Crossing from Providence
To Newport

Cresting the Claiborne Pell Bridge, I drive
straight into the pearly sunrise,
where one planet pulses clear
as a holy promise. Sailboats
moored to left and right ride
the iridescence of Narragansett Bay
on which a cruise ship floats
in tiers like a wedding cake.

What promises I used to see
in such a sight, before your body
drew into a claw, nurses drew
your blood, punctured your scalp
with the crown and Gamma Knife.

Now I come to see your daughter
married. When you heard "cancer"
your great grief was for your absence
here. But this bride's day
will rise to noon, and the world
gives what it gives: my eyes
are mine, but see
through yours as well.

The Blessing

Your seizures began under your bedside lamp
as you lay reading as if it were an ordinary night.
But on the nightstand, the bottles of pills: Ritalin,
Tegratol, Proscar, Cepra, Colace, Temazepam.
"Something is happening," you said, and a corner
of your mouth drooped; your left eye quivered and
closed. Spasms marched across your fingers one by
one, then up your arm, into your face. I helped you
step into your khakis, buttoned up your shirt.
Under a spell, one foot in front of the other, we left

the bedroom—you, for the last time. As if
it were any Saturday night, we drove to Lexington,
drew up to the emergency room. When its glass
door slid open before us, we entered disaster's
gathering place: a man held a paper towel to his
bleeding forehead, his wife begged into a cell
phone for her mother to keep the kids just
till she could come first thing in the morning.
A whole family, tight-lipped, pale, sat and stood
around a man, his coat pulled up to hide his face.

A skinny girl, alone, rocking, shushing a limp baby,
stared anxiously at the fluorescent window
where help might call her name. Half a dozen
school boys rehearsed in awed voices
the process of their wreck that slung their buddy out
onto the pavement. A peckish, red-cheeked toddler

pulled away from her exhausted mother. At last
the window opened just a crack to let your name
come out. Finally behind the glass, we, in a tongue
learned at check-ups and check-ins, recited

the litany: melanoma, metastases, gamma knife,
bio-chemotherapy, interferon, whole-brain radiation,
—dreamily, as if this weren't your own self's
body: your calloused, useful hands; your quick eyes
that saw pictures in the world; the ladder of your back
that could raise and fling a sack of horse-feed heavier
than a man. A nurse led you to a hallway cot (all cubicles
full of hurt already). I pulled close a chair, tried to keep
the passage clear, gripped your softening hand,
tried to think what else you might have to do without.

Invisible behind a curtain, a baby set up
his primal cry, raw as a fresh-pulled root.
The doctor told the young parents to bathe him
in cool water, assured them his fever would go
down by morning. He would not die. And still
the baby wailed. Your own face dropped its pain,
its fear, and you smiled a smile clear as good
water. "His life is just beginning. Mine is
almost done," you said. "I just hope his will be
half as rich as mine has been for me."

In the Japanese Garden at Asticou Inn

Northeast, Maine

You would have loved this careful place. We
might have sat on the bench by the pond
among the spirea and azaleas. But
your heavy absence is shaggy as the rock
I see through ripples on the water,

wedged in silt, silvered in sunlight,
big as a man, all but invisible, glistening
like the muscles of the summer boys down on
their knees snipping shoots of grass, and
rearranging whitish pebbles on the narrow path.

My Screensaver

I would never have put the picture there
because my teeth and nose are big,
but my daughter likes this photograph of you
in your bright red sweater, of me in my sunny wool.
I do admit I love seeing, as the screen lights,
the brightness in your eyes at holding me
and the happiness in my own at being
in the circle of your arms. Outside

the bank of floor-length windows
in your dining room, the Christmas
snow lies cold behind us, and, over your
shoulder, frozen in tableau against a backdrop
of bare vines and tree trunks, unbeknownst
to us six deer: two does, a stag, three
fawns, all heads lifted from icy
tufts of grass to regard our

strangeness as we sit down
to feast. In the lightning of this
moment two worlds are one: their
wilderness in which your death is moot; our
ritual frozen in the glass. The deer,
foraging, struck as still at us as
we at them. Someone
pulls out a chair.

The spell breaks. They
vanish instantly into the

trees and snow, stirring a
small white smoke behind each hoof
as they leap into their
journey deep
inside this
picture.

Intensive Care, Oncology

Swept up in our own storm, still we registered
the fact of Hurricane Katrina aimed like a
gun to rip New Orleans. The television,
incessantly updating, floated like a window
by Magritte in the air above your bed. Next
morning, your treatment starting, we could be
happy that the levies held the surge. You then
lay flat, as ordered, tubes plugged into your port,

felt briefly, finally, like yourself as nurses
loosed the poisonous current in your blood.
By your bed, anchored to your hand (still useful,
calloused), I watched the riptide push you
under. One moment you were
there; the next, in watery fluorescent light
your body lay as empty of yourself as your
shoes and jacket in the wardrobe by the sink.

Why Marriage Works

Nothing you want from me.
Nothing I need from you.
Satisfied now
with what we have given,
what we have gotten,
we lie sleep-heavy,
notched to the other,
the struggle forgotten.

The Lamp

The new moon, the ghost of a ghost, floats
below the surface in a cold sea
of cloud. When you died after months
of longing, the moon was full, and I still
felt the holiness of your presence
in the room where the long chain
of your breath broke. For days after,
you made the lamp, untouched, light,
and then go dark. I was spent, afraid, full
of you, your absence. And I unplugged
the lamp. Now, of course, I long
for any sliver of poor light.

IV

At Auction, July 3, 1970

For Lucy

You lay in the curve of my belly;
the morning glistened around us.
Across the dappled yard the contents
of the empty house were spread:
gleaming walnut dressers, cherry
tables, chairs of all sorts
under the trees in front; out back,
on wagon beds lay tools, jars, pots
and pans, round boxes of felt hats—
the bones of a life turned out
of drawers, shelves, cupboards,
as if ransacked by a burglar.

My father, my mother, happy
at your coming birth, sat
with me in the tent. The auctioneer
sang his song of numbers, of beauties
that he offered, of usefulness, desire.
We whispered to each other, shyly
signaled our bids. Sometimes we rose,
stepped into sun to inspect a table,
a Shaker basket, a scrap
of fabric in a box, then came back
to report, or bring a tuna sandwich,
or a cup of icy tea. We planned
our picnic for the Fourth.

Younger than I am now, my parents
helping me furnish my new marriage,
bought a tall, rough basket,
still in my study; a tin picture
of gay-nineties girls;
a Windsor chair now
broken in my basement.
I was full of prospects; their hopes
renewed through me, through you:
my clear years of duty
set to start; my mother's
wordless knowledge of this simplicity.

The stuff of someone's life
lay all around us on the grass.
The malignancies of age
hadn't gripped my parents;
the fractiousness of marriage
hadn't come to me
on that fiery July third
when those distant sorrows rose
invisibly before our eyes,
burst above us like Roman candles,
falling to earth in graceful, darkening curves.

Breath

You wake up sad every morning after age 35.
                                        —David Shields

The chain recedes unbroken to my mother,
to hers, to hers, back, back, and back
like the image of a mirror in a mirror
in a mirror, until the eye can't see them.
My daughter, ripe as a peach at its one
moment, learned the rhythm of my breaths
curled beneath my ribs where she grew like
Alice on the magic teacake of my flesh.
She outgrew her tiny room and, thrust out,
took up the breaths that built her. Linked
we breathe together for awhile. But now
I stiffen, my skin evaporates like the sea
whereon a convoy of white sails
slips one by one over the horizon.

In the First Hours of Your Life

(Andrew Vance Seligson, January 27, 2008)

I am a cliché. Grandmother: stiff, good,
half-deaf, bloodless as a greeting card.
But these many states away, I feel you burst
the darkness of my daughter's womb, butting
through the gate of bone into the light, drawing
after you the blood-filled sac you grew in.

In this first hour of your life I think
of much-loved bodies fallen back to darkness,
whose blood is quick and fresh in your new
veins, in you whose flesh re-gathers theirs.

In your first hour I think about your
last, and pray those gates of horn swing
gently for you, finished with your life, not
easy (because it was a human life),
but filled with sunshine on your face,
snow in wakes around your quiet footsteps,
and spills of rain on fields you walked in.

In your first hour I am far away,
but, more than sentimental yearnings,
I am a body, once new as yours.
My old flesh hungers now to hurry
to you, to behold black depths
in your astonished eyes, starving
for the light, in your first hour.

Andy's Breath

Sweet cloud that I breathe in, lying beside you,
easing you over the threshold from the bright day
of things to run toward, to greet with happy
shouts, into the dark closed room of night,
where wonder blackens, and strange stillness
falls upon you as the comforter sleep settles
on the nugget of all you might become.

As hungry as a patient is for gas
that eases pain, I will inhale your breath
until dreams bloom behind your eyes
and scatter night, like golden pollen, across
the world you know so far. Upon my face
your breath like air perfumed
by tropic flowers refreshes me
as the body of the girl-child renews
the ancient caliph she sleeps beside. Subtle
as the wake of butterflies, your breath
stirs molecules across the earth, moves
particles within the stars, is stronger
than a hemp rope, and connects us,
you and me, to Eve and Adam in that first,
most fragrant garden.

Once, my breath chain broke (a medical procedure
gone awry), but was mended by a doctor's pounding
on my chest. And though your breaths, caramel

tonight, and sure as life itself, will also one day falter,
I'll breathe them now, before I leave your darkened
room, as avid as the addict for the smoke, the powder.

My Grown Daughters Asleep
in the Same Bed

Curling together as they did as children,
they now sleep peacefully, like twins
jigsawed in the womb. Earlier tonight,
the first crisis of Susannah's engagement,
new, surprising pains shooting along the wires
to California: her impulsive purchase
of a car. From the next room
Lucy and I heard her crying to the phone.
Lucy leaned against me and I held her tight.
"There are such hard things," I lamely said.
"Yes, there are," said Lucy,
"but the good outweighs the bad,
doesn't it?" I feel her old small shape,
her sister's, too, against my body.
Quiet fell beyond the shut door.
I said the prayer, "Yes."

Disappointing the Dead

In front of my father, I told his doctor that I thought
his treatments should be stopped. "What do we do,
then," my father faced me, unbelieving, "just nothing?"

On my mother's last morning I went to the "Y," not
to her nursing home. In the afternoon, I postponed
until Sister Christina called, "A stroke," she said.

In her journal, forty years before I read it, Mother
agreed with Daddy that they should not help me
as they did my brother because they disapproved
the hippie way we lived.

My cousin told me yesterday that when, new married,
I told my parents at the supper table that I registered
Democrat, my father cried when he told Aunt Grace.

On Uncle Bradley's porch, in the sunshine of his last
spring, he asked how I liked my new teaching job.
I, half-hearted, said, "It's okay." "Well it's a job,
at least," he said.

I purposed always to visit Donna, but the time was
never right (my busy days, her husband's rules). "Why
does only Judy come, and Mary Ann?" she asked.

And Bill, in his last week, asked for his small pillow.
So thick the wall I hid behind, I had no notion what

he wanted. I sang to him days later, stroked his face,
his arm. He could not speak. He pushed my hand down
where I wouldn't let it go.

Such fuss. The failure of word, of touch, of presence.
Such hurt, to disappoint the dead.

A Nap in Summer

The cicadas' song swerves this way and that.
My eyes, fallen shut, open, my head at the foot
of the bed in the leaf-green shade of my room.
The clock stands at 10 a.m. On the table, a photograph
of Bill sitting on the floor, looking up, pieta-like,
cradling his grandson. Above the alabaster
lamp, a watercolor by my student, "Mr. Brown Steps
Out Tonight," his knee drawn high in dance beneath
an alabaster moon. And, in a picture, Jake, just
foisted onto a mantel by hands all but invisible at his
waist. On his first birthday, an iridescent cone juts
from his head, above the clock. Over the headboard,
Mary Gentry's tapestry, dark as a door, opens onto
a forest floor where two stags pose, one close,
the other far. Beneath his chandelier of horn,
the near one's eye levels at me a gaze most human.
Behind him winds a path of light that drops beyond
the ridge, falls out of sight among the shrunken trees.

Sleeping in the Bed with Jake, My Grandson, Three Years Old

You curl backward in the curve of my body,
your head under my nose, your fresh body
hot as a sausage, your scent flaming from
your scalp, the roots of your hair, and I revel
as in a flower, its petal licking my nostrils.

My sleep beside your sleep lightens when you
pitch yourself around in bed like a sparking
pinwheel's pleasure in itself, or a puzzle
piece shifting for its own fit.

I wake near dawn because the round
stone of your head butts against my back,
its deep heat burning through my gown.
That fire sunk in the rock of yourself
will not gutter until I've long gone
dark and cold. Even then those tongues,
orange and indigo, may sometimes say
my name.

At Newark Airport, Looking Toward Mecca

At sunset, outside Terminal A, cabbies wait
their turn, their taxis idling in a line, to pick up
travelers they'll carry homeward. Meanwhile,
they pray: the low sun gilds the chain-link fence
that bounds the tarmac, backlights the six dark men
straight and beautiful amongst the fumes, arms folded
at their waists. One stands in front and leads
as he might a line of dancers, all bow as he does,
at the neck, the waist, the hip, then all fall upon
their knees, their faces singing into oily earth.

They supplicate and praise in unison, above
the bourdon of many motors, in ancient syllables
more guttural than my ear knows. Their descant
interrupts the sky, its darkening bowl broken
at its rim by the dying fire of the God that made
this place where water stands in dirty rainbows.

They rise from their prostration on the asphalt,
faces clear, oblivious to this reduction of creation,
this declension of Allah's work. Meanwhile,
planes caterwaul like threatened beasts struggling
to break free of this scarred planet's hold. At last
they lift, and quiet as they go, crisscross the sky
into the night. All that has been: here and holy.

Acknowledgments

First and foremost, I wish to thank Jane Gentry Vance's daughters, Susannah Gopalan and Lucy Seligson, on behalf of all who share with them a deep appreciation for the work of their mother. Grateful acknowledgments are due to the staff of the University Press of Kentucky—especially Steve Wrinn, Patrick O'Dowd, Leila Salisbury, and Ashley Runyon—for publishing this collection and guiding it through the early publishing process; to David Cobb and Pat Gonzales—for their meticulous care during the editing and production stages; and to Mack McCormick and Jackie Wilson for the promotion of the collection. I also wish to thank MaryKatherine Callaway, director of Louisiana State University Press, for permitting the republication of *A Garden in Kentucky* and *Portrait of the Artist as a White Pig,* and Jonathan Allison, Angela Ball, R. H. W. Dillard, Mary Ann Taylor-Hall, Pearl James, Sylvia Wilkinson, and Lisa Williams for their continued support and valuable editorial contributions throughout this project.

Title Index

Index of First Lines

Rain falls on the roof, 204
Rows of new homes, tidy in plastic siding, come, 106

Safe at home today, making my rounds, 153
See her now as she was then, 159
September sun checkers his yard, 17
She goes blind down the aisle, 7
Spring was your last season. Now it's here, 262
Sun pools, 14
. . . sustains only a small poem, 31
Sweet cloud that I breathe in, lying beside you, 281
Swept up in our own storm, still we registered, 271

That face of mine looks me straight in the eye, 187
That spring there were floods, 53
The bass of the thunder, 99
The body asks its own questions, 63
The canal blackens under the sunset, 72
The chain recedes unbroken to my mother, 279
The cicadas' song swerves this way and that, 286
The day falls open out of the sky, 164
The first blue sky since December, 75
The flames ate the house from the bottom up, 80
The maple's green, 190
The mud of January, 67
The new moon, the ghost of a ghost, floats, 273
The rooms of Mother's house shone, 118
The simple sun can shine Kentucky bright, 229
The temperature is five above, 48
The white clouds stacked on the horizon, 160
The woman stands in shadow thick as night, 235
Thin clouds work the sheet of sky, 16
Thirty years and it will be a different picture, 29
This room is too small, 237
Through skeins of sleep I hear my cat, 195
Today I wash my windows inside, 47
To have a task that takes you, 91
To know what it wants, 64
Tonight I go to sleep to thunder over the fields, 117
Tonight snow, 39
To tell the young about the country you've crossed into, 232
Two by two, as orderly as the ark, as close, 242
Two hundred years ago, near the gash of earth called, 243